WITHDRAWN

EMBROIDERED
EFFECTS

EMBROIDERED EFFECTS

Projects and Patterns to Inspire Your Stitching

◇◇◇◇◇

BY *Jenny Hart*

PHOTOGRAPHS BY *Aimée Herring*

◇◇◇◇◇

CHRONICLE BOOKS
SAN FRANCISCO

Library of Congress Cataloging-in-Publication Data:
Hart, Jenny, 1972–
    Embroidered effects : projects and patterns to inspire your stitching / by Jenny Hart.
        p. cm.
    Includes bibliographical references and index.
    ISBN: 978-0-8118-6701-6
    1. Embroidery. 2. Embroidery—Patterns. I. Title.

TT770.H28 2009
746.44'041—dc22

2008044780

Embroidery and illustrations by Jenny Hart.

Manufactured in China
Designed by Design Army

Sublime Stitching is a registered trademark of Sublime Stitching LLC

10 9 8 7 6 5 4 3 2 1

Chronicle Books LLC
680 Second Street
San Francisco, California 94107

www.chroniclebooks.com

Contents

PROJECTS

INTRODUCTION

EMBROIDERY IS ENDLESSLY INSPIRING. When I began my exploration of embroidery less than ten years ago, I was constantly craving something new to make with my hands and mind working in tandem (staring at a computer screen and typing doesn't count). I had always loved the look of embroidery, but didn't think I could possibly sit still long enough to do it. I was foolish enough to not try it for many years, thinking it was probably too difficult, too boring, too tedious, and, well, just not my thing.

But then I began noticing it more and more everywhere. And then I wanted to see it everywhere it wasn't. When I began stitching for the first time I felt my entire world slow down, which was a very good thing. For anyone who already knows the joy of needleworking, this is hardly a revelation. But it really was a surprise to me, especially after expecting the opposite experience of frustration or tedium. You see, I put off learning to embroider for a long time, only admiring it for years with an oh-I-could-never-do-*that* mentality. But I needed something new to work with my hands. Gosh, what could that possibly be?

Embroidery seemed to be slipping away into the past. And each time I'd come across it, on vintage linens or my grandmother's tea towels, it felt like finding an old photo of a former beauty, glorious in a heyday from long ago, who was today forgotten and aged from neglect.

My eyes started seeking out hand-worked decorative stitching wherever possible. I had never really done much needlework in my life and had never taken an interest in it before. But over several years I began admiring it. Never trying it, just loving it. Bright colors stitched on white cottons, sometimes with an endearingly awkward hand, looked like lost orphans that I wanted to take home with me (and often have, far too many times!). It seems as though most who begin a successful romance with stitching remain in love with it for the rest of their lives. My affection for it hasn't waned . . .

GETTING STARTED AND USING THIS BOOK

BEFORE I LEARNED TO EMBROIDER, the biggest obstacle for me was simply learning how. I didn't sew, or really know anyone who did needlework. Turning to books was intimidating: the best embroidery books are those that have been reprinted for decades and contain hundreds of diagrams of complex, must-be-worked-this-way stitches. But because these books were written for a previous generation who grew up sewing (and can make heads or tails of a diagram faster than I can), the basics are sometimes quickly skimmed over, or not included at all. That's why I like to cover the starting points for those who may be trying embroidery for the first time, even if you're not. Embroidery is a vast subject that expands into realms that I won't even be able to venture into here. My goal is to get you past the basics and into your own inspiration by providing a wide array of tools and techniques that will keep you stitching well beyond the projects in this book. You'll find the basic stitches reviewed along with variations, combinations, and alternate applications. Books on embroidery can be intimidating, so rather than bombard you with a gazillion stitches, I wanted to give you a little bit of everything all in one book. From

Embroidery Today

EMBROIDERY NEVER DIES: it just keeps coming back better and more beautiful than before. And it's been enjoying a glorious revival in popularity. Even for this millennia-old needlecraft, new innovations, methods, and ideas continue to arise. Because of embroidery's illustrative possibilities it's easy to keep it fresh and contemporary with current and popular motifs. But that hadn't happened for a good long time, as embroidery designs slipped into endless re-workings of old-timey designs and country-cutesy motifs. Not since the Victorian rage of crazy quilting or the revival of textile arts and crafts in the '70s has American embroidery enjoyed popular new approaches like it does today. You have new options for patterns, and improved tools and resources abound. Embroidery's been shaken up a bit, and advanced into the 21st century. Hmm. I wonder what its next incarnation will be . . .

front to back, the tools, fabrics, techniques, stitches, and tips should bring you comfortably to the 21 projects designed to inspire you.

I also hope this book will become a resource that you can return to again and again for ideas, projects, and information. Not just precise how-tos, but ideas you can expand on and apply in your own, creative way. I also hope you'll turn to friends and family or seek out others who stitch to help troubleshoot anything that might not make sense. And that's the best way to learn embroidery, which is why it has been taught that way for so long—with someone showing you how. There's no substitute for one-on-one lessons, so seek a stitcher out.

When I began working in embroidery I turned to books to learn more, not knowing anyone immediately around who could get me started. Many of the best needlework books from decades past are no longer in print, and looking for them can be a rewarding hunt for sometimes-obscure information. I've collected rare and out-of-print needlework books for years and have noticed something interesting about how they differ. For most of its very long life (dating back thousands of years), embroidery has been an oral tradition, being taught from person to person without techniques being written down, or written down with the author's unique perspective. This is why if you've ever looked at several books on embroidery, they may describe the same techniques differently, or use different names for the very same stitches. This is what makes embroidery so fascinating, and open to innovation and your personal touch. This is also why I don't like to get overly involved with the "must-do" approach for teaching embroidery, with strict standards of perfection expected from your first stitches. All embroiderers have their preferences, their own style, and techniques differ from country to country and stitcher to stitcher. After all, it's innovation and change that allows creativity to flourish. We all have more fun when there's room to play and experiment, make mistakes and try new things. The most inspired ideas arise from those moments. So, don't worry too much about doing things the "right" way or the "wrong" way. If you're happy with the results and enjoy yourself, it means you're doing it right. Respected tradition provides the groundwork here, but let's see if new, inspired traditions can take shape with you to keep embroidery alive and well.

Most who begin a successful romance with

STITC

HING

remain in love with it for the rest of their lives

matters most is that it feels good in your hand, and will allow the thread to pass easily through the fabric. If your thread stops suddenly when the eye of your needle reaches the fabric, you're likely working with too thick thread on too slim of a needle.

Generally speaking, there are three types of needles used for embroidery: **crewel, chenille, and tapestry**. Crewel needles are sharp; chenille needles are also sharp, but longer (with a larger eye for stitching with heavier threads); and tapestry needles are blunt. You'd use a tapestry needle when working on an even-weave fabric (see page 29) to avoid piercing the weave at any point other than the intersection of the weave. Needles are numbered to indicate their size, or gauge: 1 to 10 for crewel, and 14 to 26 for chenille and tapestry. The higher the number, the slimmer the needle. Use a slim needle for working with fine threads, a larger needle for more open weaves and thicker thread.

Is the needle catching or stopping when you try to pierce your fabric? Does it seem like it shouldn't be doing that? It might be a difficult or irregular weave, or it might be another mysterious culprit: a metal burr. Run your thumb and forefinger down the length of your needle to its tip, and see if you feel an irregularity in the finish. A tiny, microscopic piece of the metallic finish (a manufacturing defect) might be the thing catching on your fibers as you work. This happens occasionally and you'll want to get a new needle.

Is the finish on your needle wearing off? Sometimes skin chemistry doesn't go well with certain types of metal coatings on needles. Some needles are coated in nickel, others in platinum. If you find a needle's finish is irritating your skin or rubbing off, you might want to switch to platinum. Call your local specialty needlework store and they can help you find specialty needles in different finishes.

SCISSORS

I HAVE A SMALL CONFESSION TO MAKE. One of the reasons I took up embroidery was so I had a legitimate reason to own a pair of golden crane scissors. Long before embroidery caught my eye, this whimsical and beautiful scissor design attracted my attention with its perfect incorporation of elegant bird and essential tool. The tools for embroidery tend to be rather humble and simple, so there's not a lot of need for expensive anything to show off in your sewing room, but you can indulge in fancy scissors. And, to be fair, special embroidery scissors are a necessity. You'll need a fine, sharp tip that's designed for easily snipping tiny threads and uprooting errant stitches. So pick out a pair you really love and don't let a soul use them for anything other than their intended purpose (that means: not for cutting paper, fabric, or other craft projects). You won't be able to substitute household scissors for your stitching work!

FLOSSES AND THREADS

A COLLECTION OF COLORFUL FLOSSES will provide your paintbox for embroidery. Anything you can thread on your needle and pass through your fabric is game, but here are some of the most commonly found threads for embroidering (without going into specific threads designed for tapestry, crewel, or other types of embroidery). What you stitch with will depend on your project and the look you want to achieve: fine detail or chunky stitches? Shimmery shine or matte finish? It's up to you.

SIX-STRAND FLOSS:

This thread is made up of six tiny strands that you can separate for finer detail. The number of strands is also referred to as a "ply." Some project instructions may suggest working in "three ply," or three strands only, for a specific area of a design to maintain detail. Six-strand embroidery floss is inexpensive, easy to work with, abundantly available, and comes in endless color choices. Usually 100-percent cotton (but also available in rayon and silk), stranded floss is colorfast so you can wash it and wear it. Most of the projects in this book are made with six-strand cotton floss. Nothing fancy. These are sold as "skeins," which are coiled bundles held together by paper bands. There are two tails extending from the coil. One is supposed to allow you to pull freely from the skein, and the other won't. It often seems to me that pulling either tail results in snagging and a tangly mess. If you remove the bands to re-organize your floss (I always do), be sure to keep track of the floss color number in case you want to know which colors you've used and want to replace them. You can re-wrap the floss on flat card "bobbins," put them in small plastic bags, or tuck tidily into sectioned craft boxes. Me? I re-wrap the floss around three fingers and plop the coil on a spindle rack designed to hold spools of thread. It's not fussy, and I don't keep track of floss color numbers this way, but I can see all my colors easily and grab what I need when I want to switch colors.

PERL COTTON:

This is a 100-percent cotton cousin to six-strand. Perl cotton (see sidebar on the facing page for various spellings of "perl") is typically two lightly wound, non-divisible threads, like fine yarn, which means you won't be able to separate it or divide it before or during stitching (to separate away strands or use with split stitch). **It comes in three different thicknesses or weights: 3, 5, and 8 (with 8 being the finest).** Vintage linens with small detailed work, where you can barely tell where a stitch starts and stops, usually were made with fine perl cottons. Sold in skeins and balls.

COTON À BRODER:

That's a fancy French moniker for a very humble and plain thread. Pronounced *cotton uh bro-DAY*, this is a finer thread, made up of four- or five-ply cotton, that is durable and colorfast. Unlike perl cotton, it has a dull, matte finish. At first glance you might not notice the difference between this and a skein of six-strand embroidery floss (but now you know what it is).

RAYON FLOSS:

When you go shopping for threads, your attention may be drawn to those lovely pearlescent skeins of rayon. They create extremely shiny, light-reflecting stitches that will mesmerize. By all means give them a try, but let me prepare you for how difficult and slippery they can be to work with. These glossy strands don't like to hold their place, even once they're worked on fabric, making it difficult to create tidy stitches that stay. Don't let me prevent you from trying them, but be aware that sometimes pretty is a pain!

VARIEGATED AND OVERDYED FLOSS:

Variegated floss is dyed in such a way that the color's hue goes from light to dark along the length of the strands (sorta like tie-dye). For example, red variegated will go from dark red to deep pink to light pink to soft pink and back again. All you have to do is stitch and your design will have a range of hues in the same color, appearing in one design. This can give a really nice effect, lending the appearing of incorporating different shades of floss, without have to actually re-load your needle. Variegated floss is usually consistent in the length a certain hue appears before it changes again, so if you are working on a counted, gridded pattern and trying to predict where that dark blue will show up, you can reasonably plan ahead. Overdyed threads are similar to variegated, with the differences being they may incorporate multiple colors on one skein, are usually hand-dyed (be sure to test for color fastness), and don't maintain the same consistency in where the colors change. Overdyed threads offer

Merciful
MERCERIZED COTTON!

MERCERIZED COTTON? What's that? You'll see the word "mercerized" on lots of available cotton threads. This is a manufacturing process developed in the mid-nineteenth century by John Mercer as a way to strengthen cotton fibers and produce a shiny luster. This method can be applied to any cotton threads, but is most often used on what are called perl threads (a.k.a pearl, pearle, or perle). It's just a manufacturer's way of telling you this thread has gone through processing to make it strong and shiny!

{DON'T} *Let It Bleed*

COLORFAST? The majority of threads on the market are offered as being colorfast, which means they won't bleed in the wash. This is not always the case, however. If you venture off into threads made by smaller or independent manufacturers be sure to ask about the dyes used (they won't be offended, they want stitchers to know what to expect from using their threads). There are wonderful colors and fine fibers offered in small batches from independent producers that are well worth investing in. You'll just need to make sure their beauty doesn't come out in the wash. A quick and easy way to test is by dabbing a wet cotton ball against the thread to see if any color comes off on it.

Prep School for Floss

YOU MIGHT WANT to prep your floss before you begin stitching with it. It can help keep your stitches working smoothly and lying nicely without any interruptions (like snagging or tangling). You can "strip" stranded floss with Velcro to ensure all the strands are separated and neatly aligned. You may also use different types of conditioners, such as beeswax for strengthening fibers, or silicone for smoothing and easier gliding through fabric.

less predictable, but no less gorgeous, results. If you work a satin stitch with overdyes or variegated threads, you can produce a mottled look (also see "floss blending," page 81) to a solidly stitched area. You can also experiment further by separating variegated strands (for example, three from six that go red to pink), reversing the color direction of half the strands (pink to red), and re-combining them for stitching.

METALLICS AND METAL THREADS:

We like shiny things, don't we? Sadly, the majority of metallic threads don't play well with soft fibers (which makes sense if you think about it). They tend to snag and fight with cotton weaves, disrupting what should be an enjoyable experience. But that's really no reason to completely avoid them. This is when it will be worth the effort to seek out an independent needlework shop and explore their inventory of specialty threads. Also, you might look at threads not specifically designed for embroidery to use. Just because it doesn't say it's for embroidery doesn't necessarily mean you can't stitch with it! There are soft, workable threads available that have a mix of glint to them designed for other needlecrafts like lace crochet. My experience has told me that no metallics are entirely snag-proof, but some get along better with fibers than others. Try different threads available and experiment. Here's a secret when seeking stitchable metallics: have a look at ribbon. No, not that kind of ribbon . . . read on!

RIBBON:

You might notice that some threads for needleworking are called "ribbon" but don't really look like ribbon at all. These are simply flat (think dental floss), non-divisible threads that are more often used for needlepoint or counted cross-stitch. But hey—free embroiderers can play with them too! Ribbon generally comes in a far wider range of metallics, so if metallics are what you're after, check out ribbon (see Resources, page 150). Apart from this type of ribbon, there is a school of embroidery called "ribbon embroidery" that makes use of actual, narrow ribbons to create wonderful, sculptured stitches. Look into it! You'll be amazed at what can be done.

Next . . .

FABRICS & GROUNDS

WHAT ARE YOU GONNA STITCH ON?

Textiles · Paper · Screens

Say there, what are you gonna stitch on? Well, it doesn't always have to be fabric, and far be it from me to say where (or what) you can and can't stitch. Anything that you stitch on is called a "ground." It's your blank canvas (sometimes it actually might be canvas) upon which you will bestow your inspired needleworkery. There are fabrics and grounds that have weaves intended for needlework, but nothing says you can't put your stitches on other surfaces. Let's first look at the most obvious and easy places for your embroidery, and then we'll look at some not-so-obvious choices.

FINISHED TEXTILES

FINISHED TEXTILES, LIKE TABLECLOTHS, shirts, or skirts, are often what serve as inspiration. Once you start stitching, you won't be able to pass a blank textile without thinking "Oh, some stitches along here would look just so nice. . . . " One advantage of embroidering on a finished piece is that you can fit your design to suit its shape, and immediately use the textile after it's been stitched. If you sew, you have an even greater advantage of being able to work on fabric sections before you piece them together.

Many finished textiles are designed specifically for embroidery, but unfortunately don't serve their other utilitarian purpose quite as well. We've all seen those bibs that don't look like they'd do much to prevent food from getting all over baby. This is where trial-and-error and experimenting will be in your hands as you tackle available textiles around you for embroidery.

Oh, and what about T-shirts? Grrr, T-shirt fabric. Seems as soon as people pick up needle and thread, they head for the T-shirts, perhaps not knowing how aggravating they can be to stitch on. T-shirt fabric is spongy, stretchy, and has a very small, tight knit (not a weave) that makes it nearly impossible to work on without swearing and major frustration (just me?). T-shirt fabric is nearly impossible to stitch without a good stabilizer. It can also be difficult to trace a design directly onto a T-shirt with tissue-thin carbon papers (iron-on transfers work just fine) because the soft fabric doesn't provide a smooth or hard enough ground. When you simply must stitch that T-shirt, be sure to read about stabilizers (page 34) and transfer techniques (page 38) in the next section. If you are embroidering for the first time, I strongly advise you don't make working on a T-shirt your first project.

PLAIN WEAVE

SEEMS EMBROIDERY STITCHES MOST OFTEN find themselves on the simple cottons available at home. In ye olden days, you wouldn't find a proper home without stitched aprons, pillowcases, curtains, vanity runners, guest towels, tablecloths, tea towels, tea cozies . . . everything had to be stitched. Most often these cottons are plain weaves, which means the weave and weft are irregular and you won't need to pay attention to your needle entering and exiting right at the intersection where they meet. The fabric will be too fine for that, and you can just stitch up a storm. This is probably why most free embroidery ("free" meaning not dictated by the weave where your needle can and can't go) winds up on these welcoming, easy-to-work fabrics. All you have to do is use a sharp needle that will easily pass through with your thread and you're set to stitch. Sometimes running the fabric through a warm wash (skip the dryer) will help prep it for stitching by softening the fibers and slightly opening up the weave.

EVEN-WEAVE

EVEN-WEAVE FABRIC IS USED MOST often when working in counted cross-stitch. Even-weave fabrics, like aida cloth, have a consistent number, or count, of intersections per inch. So, a 14-count aida cloth will have 14 holes, or intersections, per inch. When stitching, your needle will always exit at the gap between the weave and the weft, and never through the fibers themselves.

OPEN-WEAVE AND CANVAS

OTHER TYPES OF NEEDLEWORK, like needlepoint or latch-hooking, make use of an open-weave, or canvas, which will be completely covered in stitches, so no ground is visible at all.

SATIN

EMBROIDERY ON SATIN is one of my favorites looks. I love how colorful, plain cotton floss looks surrounded by this shiny, glossy ground. You'll have to use caution, though, because the surface is very easily marred. A hoop is necessary for working on satin since it's slippery, but you'll want to be extra careful not to distort the threads of the fabric, which will look like bare spots when you remove it from your hoop. If this happens, take your fingers and massage the fibers back into place with your fingertips. I can't guarantee it will solve the problem, but sometimes it is possible to move the fibers back where they belong. Be gentle when putting it on your hoop, and don't think you'll be able to just iron out that hoop-ring afterward. Satin is typically polyester, and an overly hot iron will melt it (it will permanently wrinkle and buckle if your iron is too hot), more easily than you may think. So, when ironing satins, keep that iron at a low setting.

Weave & Weft
{A.K.A., WARP & WOOF}

◇◇◇◇◇◇◇◇◇◇◇◇◇◇◇◇◇◇

THE ABILITY TO PIERCE the surface with your needle and thread depends on the weave and the weft of the surface. The wha' and the who? Most fabrics and canvases are made up of woven fibers (okay, you know that already). The threads of a fabric that run parallel to one another, and make up the base of a fabric, are called the *weave* (or "warp"). The threads that intersect horizontally to the weave are called the *weft* (or the "woof"). I like "warp and woof" more than "weave and weft," personally. They sound like old friends with funny names.

Thoroughly confused? Don't worry about it too much. Some needleworkers make sure that the weave and weft of their fabric is kept at right angles to their work, but this is mainly a concern when working on even-weave fabrics. How do you remember which is which? Think "weft to right" as mental shorthand for "the weft runs left to right."

F-f-freezer Paper

◇◇◇◇◇◇◇◇◇◇◇◇◇◇◇◇◇◇◇◇◇◇◇◇

MANY NEEDLEWORKERS KNOW that freezer paper—that's right, the kind found in the grocery stores next to the aluminum foil—makes a quick and easy stabilizer. Who woulda thunk it? It's a roll of white paper with a light plastic coating on one side. The plastic side adheres well to fabric when ironed on as a stabilizer, and easily tears away when finished. You can also use it to back fabric that you can then run through your computer's printer (see page 100 for instructions), transferring an image directly onto the fabric. When you get to the section on creating your own designs and putting them on fabric, remember this one as an option!

Quilt Battings

◇◇◇◇◇◇◇◇◇◇◇◇◇◇◇◇◇◇◇◇◇◇◇◇

EVEN IF YOU DON'T NEED A STABILIZER or extra ground for the fabric you'll be stitching, you might want to try layering your fabric with quilt batting for added effect. Unlike batting that comes in a bag like a giant cotton puff (for stuffing pillows and toys), quilt batting is flat and sold in rolls. By layering it underneath the fabric you'll be stitching, and by stitching through both layers (you include the batting on the hoop if using one), you'll find that your stitches now have a soft, quilted look to them (without having to make a quilt). Unlike removable stabilizer, you won't remove the batting—it will stay right where it is. The added bonus is that the batting will hide any traveling stitches that might show through the front of your fabric. This works best for a project that will remain stretched and/or framed (see framing page 142). Such an easy way to add subtle, how'd-they-do-that texture to your work!

DENIM

IT WAS HUGELY POPULAR to embroider on your jeans in the '70s. Back then faded, soft jeans were more popular; today's dark, dense denims can pose a challenge for stitching. If you have your heart set on stitching your jeans, soft, broken-in ones will make for an easier time. But we all know that our needlework will look really nice on those dark ones, so we're gonna stitch them anyway. Run them through a warm wash first (using a liquid softener as an extra option), and let them drip-dry. A tumble in the dryer will only cinch up the fibers really tight, making it even tougher to stitch.

Another hurdle is accessibility to the wrong side of the fabric, because it's already sewn as a pant leg. This is why most embroidery appears down by the ankles, where it's easiest to work. If you are comfortable using the sewing technique (see page 44) you'll be able to more easily work on those hard-to-reach spots. Have a peek at the jeans project on page 130 to see another easily accessible area of your jeans that doesn't usually get stitched (the front yoke). And if you're working on the pocket, consider removing it first, stitching it, and then sewing it back on. Many pockets have been embroidered shut in their day—d'oh!

PAPER AND CARDS

THE NOVELTY OF STITCHING ON CARDS has been around since the Victorian era, when you might receive a lovely, hand-written thank-you note embellished in part with fine, silky threads, usually worked only as straight stitches, embellishing a lady's skirt or the petals of a flower. Despite how it odd it sounds, working on paper is really fun and is a charming combination of two seemingly unrelated materials. But the drawbacks are that you can't see where the needle is about to come up (we'll fix that), and if you pass your needle through a spot you didn't intend to, well, you now have a permanent hole. Experiment first: get an index card, floss up your needle, and pull a few stitches, seeing how you like it. It will be a different feel, for sure, but before you declare it too difficult, here are some things you can do to make it easier.

Take a thumbtack and prick the holes you want to stitch first, or pass your needle completely through each point you want to stitch (from front to back so the raised paper is at the backside of your card), perforating the design. This will take away the mystery of where your needle should come up, and make the actual stitching easy and fun. Just connect the dots! And don't forget that iron-on transfers can be applied to cardstock, papers, and wood.

There are also templates of decorative borders and simple designs available for pre-pricking holes on paper to stitch (see page 154).

PATTERNED FABRICS

SO OFTEN WE LOOKED AT naked fabrics as the best place for our works of stitching art, giving all the glory to the stitches and the stitches alone. But how about a playful collaboration of stitches with a patterned textile? Stitching your design over a subtle backdrop can produce a dramatic effect. There are several ways you can approach it.

One way is to apply an embroidery design over a patterned fabric and work it like you would on a plain one. This works especially well with soft patterns, like dots or gingham, that give a subtle, decorative ground. You'd be surprised how it makes your pattern look (think tattoo design over pink polka dots). And, using only one floss color lets the design stand out without competing against the colors of the fabric. Better yet, you might use your stitching to build on the fabric's existing motif and create a true interplay: how about stitching a hand holding the flower that appears on the fabric? Nice.

You can also skip the embroidery design and work only in decorative stitches that outline, embellish, or echo the fabric's existing pattern. This works best for more dramatic fabrics. For example, you might take a fabric covered in birds and flowers and outline the petals in a different color, then add metallic straight stitches to the tips of a bird's wing. Relaxing, easy, no hard planning, and the results will be charming, no matter what.

SCREEN

YES, THE KIND OF SCREEN on your doors and windows. You can embroider it. Oh yes you can! I've embroidered on a screen door before, and I'm not the only one. That screen is a canvas of wire, and if you have a screen door on your home you can really make an interesting first impression by putting some stitches there. To work a design, stick self-adhering stabilizer (see Resources, page 149) to the screen, providing a ground to stitch through. You can also buy unstretched screen at most hardware stores in metal or fiberglass. I didn't include a screen door project in this book for you, but I have done it elsewhere. A reference for working a full project on a screen door is included in the bibliography.

STABILIZERS

STABILIZERS (ALSO CALLED INTERFACING) DO JUST WHAT THEY SAY: they stabilize a fabric or ground that might not be so stitchable without them (like T-shirts). **They create a second layer that you'll stitch through at the same time as your fabric, and remove after you're finished stitching.** Some stabilizers stay put, though, like on densely embroidered patches. There are pre-made stabilizers you can buy, or you can improvise with tissue paper or beading paper.

Most prefab stabilizers have different weights (by stiffness) and different methods by which they are applied and removed. Some iron on, some stick on like a big sticker, some liquefy and brush on (and then rinse out). Some don't adhere at all; they just lie there, held in place by your hoop along with the ground fabric while you stitch through them.

Another popular stabilizer works like a filmy sheet (think of plastic wrap for food) that doesn't apply to your fabric at all, but simply gets hooped along with your ground fabric and torn away when you're finished stitching. This same type of stabilizer can be liquefied (just put some in water and let it dissolve) and brushed onto fabric. Let it dry and stiffen, then stitch. When you're finished, soak it in a bath of clean water to dissolve away (see Resources, page 149, for stabilizers).

With so many choices, it can be difficult to know which to pick. My personal preference is a medium-weight stabilizer that irons on and then pulls away. I'm not a big fan of applying adhesives of any kind to my fabrics, and never leave permanent, iron-on interfacings on my projects. This is purely a matter of personal preference, but be warned: if the product says to iron it on and leave it on, you might not be happy about it as time goes by and your embroidery doesn't age so well. Any kind of chemical adhesive that is heat-activated should be worked with only in ventilated areas, and with caution as to how the interfacing will react with your fabric.

Usually a stabilizer is applied to the wrong side of your fabric for working (especially if it's staying on after you've finished stitching), but nothing says it can't go on top. If you're putting the stabilizer on top of your fabric, it can then also be the platform for your designs. **When a dark fabric makes it hard to see the design, just put your design on the stabilizer instead of on your ground—ta daa!** Even if your fabric doesn't need a stabilizer to be stitched upon, the stabilizer can make an invisible design suddenly visible.

Because stabilizers double as grounds for designs, consider them along with the tools covered in the pattern-making section.

Also

PATTERN MAKING

INSPIRATION IS EVERYWHERE!

Pens · Transfers · Stencils

Picking out a design to embroider is what inspires most of us to get stitching. And inspiration is everywhere. From clip art to available transfers to found art in vintage coloring books to your own illustrations and musings to be translated into stitches—you can get that design ready for embroidering.

Not all designs will go directly onto your fabric. For dark fabrics, or difficult grounds (like T-shirts, silks, or anything else problematic), the design can more easily go onto a stabilizer. Even if you don't need a stabilizer, it might come in best as a ground for your design. But how do you get a design on anything?

HOT-IRON TRANSFERS

THERE'S A SECTION OF THESE waiting for you at the end of the book (be sure to read the instructions for use on page 148). Just iron the design directly onto fabric, and stitch along the lines! Hot-iron transfers are commercially offered patterns available in hundreds of motifs, but aren't as widely available as they once were. They're reusable, which means you can imprint them more than once, and makes them extremely convenient and versatile ways of getting ready-to-go designs on fabric.

If you've never used a hot-iron transfer before, I strongly suggest you test one first on scrap fabric to get used to it. I would hate for you to attempt to apply a transfer directly to an heirloom fabric, with unexpected results. Test, test!

TRACING PAPER

TRACING PAPER WILL BE YOUR FRIEND. Keep it on hand for tracing found designs before transferring them, or for laying over your fabric to work out a design for placement before you commit it to the fabric or stabilizer. An alternate is glassine, a heat-pressured paper that is a bit more substantial than tracing paper, but just as transparent. Glassine comes in larger sheets than you may find for tracing paper, and is most often used to interleave prints and photos for archival storage. Once you've traced your design onto this paper, you can use either of the following options for the next step in transferring your design.

CARBON PAPERS

CARBON PAPERS (ALSO KNOWN AS "DRESSMAKER'S CARBON") come in different colors and are commonly offered at sewing supply stores. They are laid against your fabric, with the design layered on top, and traced over with a pen or stylus. **(Tip: use a different color pen to trace over your design, like a milky gel pen, so you know where you've traced and where you haven't, avoiding any blank spots when you lift up the design).** I've found that these blue, red, or yellow chalky papers tend to produce a faint design that won't transfer easily (I have to press extra hard or repeat my lines) and often rubs off before I can finish stitching. So I started looking elsewhere for carbons, and discovered graphite-based carbon papers that leave a dark line that won't easily fade or rub off while stitching (but some are designed to be erasable or wash out when you want to remove the lines). These carbons also come in white, which is handy for dark fabrics.

The drawback of carbon papers is that they tend to be tissue-paper thin, which means they don't work well for spongy or soft fabrics like baby bibs, T-shirts, or denim. Any time you are tracing with carbon paper, you'll need a hard, smooth surface under your work so you can press evenly against the fabric. Soft fabrics are candidates for using a stabilizer with a design already on it to follow. Or the next option. . . .

TRANSFER PENS, PENCILS, AND CRAYONS

THERE ARE NUMEROUS TYPES OF TRANSFER PENS, pencils, and now crayons available. You use these by first tracing directly over a design (be sure to reverse it first!), turning the template into an iron-on. The inks are transferable, and can vary from product to product. I've found some transfer pencils that work extremely well (and others that don't) but I've had better results with pens. Working with transfer pens may take a deft hand and some practice—most of these are constructed with a retractable nib that releases the ink when you press down on the tip (like a paint marker). Be careful though, this can produce an unwanted glob of ink, leaving a fat line you can't hide with your stitches. Avoid this by pressing the ink nib on a piece of waste cloth or paper towel to get it started, rather than on your design. These pens work extremely well for transferring the designs, however, leaving a clear outline for you to follow. Worth the effort!

"Iron-Ons"

◇◇◇◇◇◇◇◇◇◇◇◇◇◇◇◇◇◇

ANY TIME THE WORD "IRON-ON" is used, don't think of it as an iron-on like you'd see on a T-shirt. Inks and papers used for transferring designs leave only the lines you'll stitch on fabric; they don't coat the entire area of your fabric with a peel-away design. That said, using ink-jet transfer papers as a way to get your design onto fabric is not one I suggest, because you'll be left with an 8.5" x 11" area covered with that peel-away film. We don't want that.

◇◇◇◇◇◇◇◇◇◇◇◇◇◇◇◇◇◇

WATER-SOLUBLE PENS

WATER-SOLUBLE PENS ARE OFTEN USED for directly marking on fabric, but don't work in the same way as a transfer pen or pencil. You would use these most often for marking guidelines. But you can also use them if you're bravely drawing freehand directly onto your fabric. They can be good to keep around, but be aware that they tend to bleed into the fibers when used, making a fuzzy, indistinct line. While they erase with water, avoid leaving them sitting on your fabric for too long, or you may find they don't want to wash out as easily. With any pen or ink that claims to be water soluble, you run the risk of a faint stain remaining. Read the instructions and always test first!

STENCILS

QUILTERS MAKE USE OF STENCILS to trace large, simple motifs on quilt blocks. Reusable and easy-to-use, pre-cut plastic stencils can be used without the need for tracing paper, transfer pens, or carbons. Just lay the stencil over the area you want to stitch, and follow the opening with a soft pencil or water-soluble pen.

POUNCING

POUNCING IS AN AGE-OLD METHOD of transferring a design to fabric. It's not the most convenient way of transferring a design, but it's stood the test of time and is helpful to learn for when no other option is available. It's done by first pricking the outline of your pattern with a needle (stick the eye end into a cork or use a thumbtack to avoid sore fingers), and laying it over the fabric (tape or weigh the design in place) and then stamping it with a loose chalk, usually loaded on a large soft brush or filled inside a little fabric pouch that lets the chalk pass through, leaving an outline of dots on your fabric. Powdered chalks are available specifically for doing this. Using a fixative of some sort might be necessary (so your design doesn't brush off easily). Yes, it's messy and probably not the method you'll be using most of the time, but it's good to have options!

An easier alternative to stamping loose chalk over a pricked design is to lay carbon transfer paper against the fabric you'll be stitching (carbon side to the stitching surface), and underneath the design you'll be pricking. When your pin pushes through the design and the carbon at the same time, it will leave a small carbon dot on the ground you'll be stitching. Just be sure to make enough pin pricks closely together to create an easy-to-follow line of dots, or you might get lost while you're stitching. We don't want you to get lost.

Next . . .

STITCHING
METHODS

THERE'S NO WRONG WAY TO WORK A STITCH

◇◇◇

Easy · Medium · Hard

There's more than one way to pull that stitch, and how you work it will depend entirely on your personal preference. Some people like to work with a hoop, others without—and that can determine what stitching method you use. In my book (both figuratively and literally), there's no wrong way to work a stitch so long as you are happy with the results and enjoying embroidering. But there are established, traditional methods that make a certain stitch what it is (and isn't) and techniques that help things go smoothly, with consistent results.

◇◇◇◇◇

AND SPEAKING OF CONSISTENCY . . . there's also a lot of rather interesting inconsistency among authorities when you try to read up on exactly how to do something in embroidery, which lends an air of excitement and mystery about stitching. It's inventive, it's personal, it's passed from person to person, and is constantly modified, altered, and reenvisioned. If you've ever looked up the same stitch in more than one embroidery dictionary, you might find that the very same stitch is worked differently but called the same thing. To me, this is the beauty of embroidery, and also why I avoid the "This is how it must be done!" attitude, which has turned off and discouraged many a potential needleworker. I don't want to get too hung up on all that jazz. I want to give you reliable information along with the freedom to play and experiment without dictating too many "musts" for your stitches (and without also completely disregarding traditional techniques at the same time). Ready? Let's stitch.

STABBING TECHNIQUE (a.k.a. Maggam)

SOUNDS KIND OF VIOLENT, DOESN'T IT? All this means is that you are working your needle in an up-and-down, one-step-at-a-time fashion. This is also known in India as maggam work. Down through the front, up through the back, down again, up *uh-gain*. . . . It may sound beginner-ish, but it really isn't. It's how I work all the time, thankyouverymuch, and this technique will give you more control, accuracy, and evenness to your stitches. This is also the easier method to use when working on a hoop. I like to work on a hoop, as a rule, and I enjoy the smooth rhythm associated with stitching by stabbing (hee hee).

SEWING TECHNIQUE

INSTEAD OF TAKING EACH POINT OF EXIT and entry one-by-one as with the stabbing technique, the needle will enter and exit the fabric in one simultaneous first step (where you may also have to yank a little harder to pass through for the last, finishing step), keeping your needle always shuttling across the top of your fabric. The benefits to working in the sewing technique are that it allows you to fluidly and quickly work certain stitches (if you're good at it—I'm not!), and lets you work on a surface where you can't reach around to the back for every completed stitch to pull the needle through. You must either not work on a hoop, or else keep your fabric loose enough on the hoop so that your fingers underneath can push the fabric upward, allowing the needle to enter and exit the fabric in one motion. Some stitches are worked best in the sewing

Needle Hand / Non-Needle Hand

SOME BASIC TERMINOLOGY: the hand that holds your needle is often referred to as your "needle hand." The hand that holds your hoop is called the "non-needle hand." Seems clear enough, yes? If you are right-handed, you will probably feel most comfortable holding your needle in your right hand, and your hoop in your left. For lefties, the inverse. Some instructions may indicate what to do with which hand—just making sure you'll know which is which!

Much Ado About Knottin'

KNOTS ON THE BACK OF YOUR FABRIC are often called out as being a grave sin. OooOoOoooh, oh *whatever*. In my humble opinion, there is far more debate and fussiness over knots than needed. There's even a popular anecdote among needleworkers about a well-known British embroiderer (with credentials from the Royal School of Needlework don'tyouknow) playfully admonishing those who are "overly concerned with their backsides." Which is to say: don't worry about it too much. The main reason you don't want to begin or end your floss with a knot is because it may produce a lump on the front of your work. Fine knots on certain weaves may pop through and, if your tail has been snipped short, could end up being a problem should it come undone and need to be resecured. But knots have never really been a true problem for me, unless they were really big, and the fabric very delicate and destined to be pressed again and again. I simply make a choice when to use a knot and when to finish with a tail.

The elegant practice of beginning and finishing work with a long tail (begin by holding the tail until you take your first couple of stitches and end by threading the tail through the backs of your stitches) is a tidy and lovely technique for finishing your embroidery. It keeps things neat and clean and hey, I make use of it all the time with my own work (along with plenty of good ol' knots). It's a good idea to keep tails tucked away to avoid a nest of loose threads back there, but knots as a means of starting or ending your floss are by no means forbidden, or the "wrong" way of doing things, at least not with me!

technique, so I encourage you to try any and all stitches both ways (except for French Knots, which don't give you a choice). You may find yourself switching back and forth between stitching styles as you work, depending on the stitch.

DOUBLE HANDED

I'M NOT SURE WHY, BUT FOR ME this technique brings to mind nuns working on oversized stretchers of embroidered allegories—probably because this technique really requires working on a large, freestanding frame so both your hands can be free at once. Here's how it works: instead of abandoning your needle as it's stuck partway through your fabric, and then reaching around behind your hoop to pull the stitch, your hands will pass the needle back and forth to each other. Kinda tough to do, actually, because your non-needle hand will take the needle and complete the stitch, and then bring the needle back up, passing it through to the front where your other hand will take the needle again. I suggest making your dominant hand the one below the surface, because you'll more easily find your exit point than by hunting with your hand you don't normally use. Try it, and you'll see what I mean. You'll need a freestanding frame to try this (or a hoop propped between your knees, which isn't very convenient). I've tried it a few times and it feels awkward at first, but it's worth giving a go to see how you like it. You'll feel so ambidextrous!

LEFT HANDED

HEY YOU, LEFTY YOU! You guys get a bum rap. It's true, there are not a lot of embroidery diagrams readily available and designed just for lefties. That's in part because the solution may be very simple: reverse the design and turn the numbers around, if you don't mind the extra time with a scanner and design program. I've often heard that looking at the design in a hand mirror helps, but that can't be ideal. I have come across some books that include sections of diagrams just for lefties and have listed them for you in the Resources (see page 151).

And we can't forget . . .

STITCH DIAGRAMS

PICK UP YOUR NEEDLE AND GIVE THEM A TRY!

Basic · Tricky · Advanced

Stitches will be your veritable brushstrokes in thread. And while most embroidery for pleasure may be worked by executing only a few simple stitches for outline (nothing wrong with that!), increasing your repertoire of fancier stitches will allow you to be more creative in embroidery and wield more textures, effects, and flourishes. We like flourishes.

BUT KNOWING WHICH STITCHES TO USE WHERE CAN POSE A CHALLENGE, especially if you're going for a certain effect, like wispy tendrils of a plant (there's a stitch for that), or shimmering water (there's a stitch for that, too). Simply learning new stitches and increasing your stitch vocabulary will give you more to say. And chances are you'll know when to say it.

I've tried to make my diagrams as simple for you to decipher as possible—**just be sure you are actually working with your floss and needle in hand to give them a try.** And be patient with yourself. I'm speaking from experience, as I taught myself each of these stitches (from books that had diagrams I sometimes stared at for hours before I could understand them). I made many errors and had to work some stitches over and over again until—CLICK!—I got it. And then, it's smooth sailing. So, get yourself a piece of play cloth (traditionally called a "doodle" cloth) to practice your stitches, and don't expect perfection with your first attempts—unless, of course, it happens!

This is how you read the diagrams: **1 indicates where your needle first comes up through the fabric from behind the hoop (also called exiting), 2 is where is goes down again (also called entering), and so on.** This is the same for diagrams showing either technique of stabbing or sewing. I also like to take things a bit further than 1-2-3. Sometimes I need more than a running start to know how to keep working a stitch, so with some of these diagrams I've completed the steps through to more than one repetition. Wherever you see numbers like 4-8-12 pointing to a single entry/exit point, no, this is not the combination to unlocking the diagram's mystery; it means that by step 8 you will be back at the same point as step 4 and you'll be back again for step 12 (same hole). You only have to follow the numbers.

The first diagrams are some of the simplest and most basic stitches, which make a great introduction to the sewing technique. Some stitches (like the good ol' French knot) can be worked only in a singular fashion. But for those stitches where you have a choice, I'll try to demonstrate both. First learning to work some basic stitches in both techniques (stabbing and sewing) will be good (and easy) practice for understanding the many variations that follow. I'll hold your hand through the more confusing ones. But I'm betting if you take the time to learn the simple ones you'll "get it" when it comes time to sew the more complicated ones.

Let's say you want to become a serious student of the stitch. You want to know definitively how a stitch is supposed to be, what it's called, what type it is, and precisely which stitch goes first and which comes next. . . . Hoo boy. Sit down. One of the fascinating things about embroidery is the diverse ways in which it is taught and carried out all over the world. One thing I know is that not all stitches fit nicely into "types" and their types might also describe their use. Some stitches themselves spawn so many variations that they become a type of stitch on their own (hello, chain stitch). Poring over piles of stitching encyclopedias in search of definitive examples can quickly become mind-boggling, and cross-referencing them as authoritative sources will produce some differing opinions. That's why I don't claim to be any sort of authority. I am merely sharing what I have learned from teachers, friends, piles of books, and my personal experience and experimentation, hoping to establish some consistency and creativity side by side.

Oh, and word to the wise: I don't recommend you read the instructions for working stitches without having a needle and thread all ready to go on your practice cloth. Seemingly complicated explanations will be oh-so-much easier to understand if you work through the steps while you read them. I'm also going to go over the sewing technique for three very basic stitches: split, stem, and back. If you've never worked the sewing technique before, I want to encourage you to give it a try. While the stabbing technique will give you more accurate, controlled stitches, the sewing technique might feel better to you (and it will help you understand diagrams you find elsewhere that use it). Enough of that? Let's learn some stitches.

Wish You Were Here

◇◇◇◇◇◇◇◇◇◇◇◇◇◇◇◇

IT'S DIFFICULT enough learning embroidery stitches from a book—imagine trying to write about them! That's my challenge. As much as I wish I could be right there to just show you in person, my best efforts will have to be with illustrations and text. It's important to follow the text for each stitch while studying the diagram (with hoop and threaded needle in hand) and reading the accompanying text at the same time. If you find yourself hopelessly confused (I hope not!), reach out and find a stitcher who would be happy to help you with that troublesome stitch in person. Also, be sure to look at the Resources, page 150, where I've included some of my favorite books on embroidery as sources for more diagrams (but don't be surprised if you find differing opinions among books on how a stitch is "supposed" to be done). I wish I could be there!

◇◇◇◇◇◇◇◇◇◇◇◇◇◇◇◇

Split Stitch

Stabbing Technique

Sewing Technique: Step 1

Sewing Technique: Step 1a

SPLIT STITCH

TYPE: *Line*
USED FOR: *Outlining, filling*

THE SPLIT STITCH GETS NO RESPECT, and is often stuck in the back of embroidery books as an afterthought instead of up front and center as a simple, useful, and lovely stitch (can you tell it's my favorite?). It's the first stitch I was taught, and is still what I use all the time for simple outlining.

1. SPLIT STITCH: STABBING TECHNIQUE

Make a single but very short straight stitch, about the length of a grain of rice. When you bring your needle back up through the fabric to make your next stitch, push your needle up through the center of the previous stitch, splitting the threads (3), and repeat, splitting each stitch you just made with the next one. See? Keep going. If you learn nothing but this one stitch, you can embroider blissfully for the rest of your life. Sometimes your floss will split nicely and evenly, making stitches that look like tiny chain stitches. The split stitch will work with six-strand floss but not perl cotton or other non-divisible threads (stem stitch will work better for that).

2. SPLIT STITCH—SEWING TECHNIQUE

Start from behind your hoop, pulling your floss all the way up. Before re-entering the fabric to make your first stitch, hold a bit of floss in place with your thumb, making a loose-ended starting stitch, and re-enter the fabric with the needle through the center of the floss you are holding (Step 1). See? You'll be coming down from the top to split the stitch (1a—the diagram shows the stitches already in progress), instead of up from behind your fabric. But hold on! Before pulling the needle all the way back down, direct the tip of the needle to exit the fabric a space ahead of where the floss has exited (2). This is when you'll want to use your fingers behind the fabric to push it up a bit to allow the needle to more easily pass. Now you can pull all the way through. The result will be a gap left with each pull of your needle that will be closed with each consecutive stitch. Repeat by returning your needle at 3. Try it this way, and see how it feels to you.

Hidden Stitch

Hidden Stitch

Hidden Stitch

⦙ HIDDEN STITCH {A.K.A. RUNNING}

TYPE: *Line*
USED FOR: *A dashed line effect, simple borders*

THIS IS THE GOOD OL' DASHED-LINE STITCH. It works particularly well by itself along the edge of fabric. Nothing says "handmade" like a hidden stitch along the hem of skirt.

Just run your needle through several folds of fabric at once to work quickly, or simply leave a space between straight stitches as you make them. Pay attention to the amount of space between each stitch if you want your stitches to be even, or just go at it and surprise yourself with the results. This is a stitch for which the sewing technique is quick 'n' dirty—but usually with uneven results. If you accordion your fabric very carefully, that will dictate more evenly spaced stitches. Otherwise, if you want perfectly spaced stitches, use the stabbing technique along a guideline.

Threading AND *Whipping*

LET'S GUSSY THIS UP A BIT. Here's a neat effect you can easily add to any of your stitches. After working a hidden stitch, take another color of floss (or the same color) and simply pass your needle along the surface of the fabric, never piercing it, up and down among the stitches you've made, like following an obstacle course in stitches. Go! Go! This is called "threading," and can be applied to many other stitches. Another similar technique is "whipping." Akin to couching (where you stitch floss around an already worked line of stitches), you'll wrap the already worked stitches around and around, over and under (instead of only underneath the stitches like threading) but never entering the fabric. It's not only applied to hidden stitches— you can whip and thread just about any worked stitch you want!

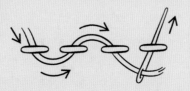

Threading

Whipping

Brick

Brick: Sewing Technique

Ripple

Zipper

⦙ BRICK

TYPE: *Line*
USED FOR: *Wider lines, filling, borders*

OKAY, I KNOW you've been very patiently going through these basic stitches, and now this one looks like just a bunch of plain ol' straight stitches lined up like bricks. Well, okay. They are. But hold up! A simple variation on this stitch will work wonders. First, let's get these bricks laid down.

Work a row of backstitches first, and then create a second and then third row, staggering your stitches to begin and end in the center of the stitch above or below. Easy enough! Now see what you can do by just loosening this stitch up a bit:

RIPPLE

If you open up your stitches, and work them in a wavy line, it makes a nice set of stitches that look like rippling water, or blowing breezes (see the Mahjong transfer pattern). Evenly lined-up stitches isn't really our goal here. Just keep them staggered and following one another. You can work this like a hidden stitch, one line at a time, or, when working the transfer pattern in the book, use the sewing technique. On your own, you can also simply draw a single curvy line on your fabric and stitch along that line with the sewing technique, producing two lines at once (see diagram at left). If you just read that and got confused, get back to your practice cloth and try it! You'll see how it works, I promise.

ZIPPER

For the countless times you've been stumped for depicting a zipper in embroidery (every day, right?), I offer this easy solution: Open, vertical brick stitches should do the trick. Looks just like a zipper, no? It can be so simple to take some basic stitches, and with just a slight variation, use them for many creative possibilities. Ah, inspiration.

Stabbing: Freeform

Stabbing: In a row

Sewing: Step 1

Sewing: Step 2

CROSS-STITCH

TYPE: *Crossed (what else?)*
USED FOR: *Borders, complete designs (counted cross-stictch), powdering, accents*

HOW'D THIS STITCH GET IN HERE? Well, it's an embroidery stitch, just like any other, one that can be used by itself or in a row according to a guideline. Counted cross-stitch is worked on fabric with an open- or even-weave that provides a grid to keep the X's neat and in their little boxes. But we're wild, go-where-we-like stitchers! So why do we want to learn the stuffy cross-stitch? Because you can use it however you like (it doesn't always have to be counted ya know), and it's the foundation for other stitches to come.

1. CROSS-STITCH: STABBING TECHNIQUE
There's really not much to explain. Just make yourself an X. If you want to make a row, guidelines will be your friend. You'll notice they start off as single lines before becoming X's. That's because when you work a row of cross-stitches in free embroidery this way, you don't have to make the X's all at once. You can first work a row of diagonal stitches (1–2, 3–4), exiting across from where you last entered the fabric. Then you come back the other way, doing the same in the opposite direction, (I like to begin working from right to left and make my second pass moving left to right, but you can start in whatever direction feels most natural to you.) Why do this? It's faster, and keeps the top stitches going in the same direction, which lends uniformity to your cute cross-stitches. Many experienced needleworkers aim for this kind of uniformity in their cross-stitches. What is it about these X's that demands such rank-and-file order?

2. CROSS-STITCH: SEWING TECHNIQUE
Even with the sewing technique, you'll be first creating a row of diagonal stitches that you'll go back and complete with a second pass coming from the other direction (time for a different color thread, anyone?). However, this type of sewing diagram always confused me, because I couldn't understand how the full X's were being made. That's because most books don't show or explain, for slow folks like me, that they're only showing the second swipe at crossing those X's. So, here are two diagrams showing you how it's done with the sewing technique in one pass, and then a second pass. Now I get it!

Twinkle

Figure 1: Ermine

Figure 2: Smyrna

☰ TWINKLE

TYPE: *Crossed or combination*
USED FOR: *Powdering, accenting*

I LOVE ACCENTING MY WORK with six-point stars. Can you believe there's not an official term for making these cute doodads? It's similar to both the *smyrna* and *ermine* stitches, but it's not quite the same (see figures 1 and 2 below to compare). It's a little more hip, with retro flair. There is a simple way to make this star that I like to call a *twinkle stitch*. Simply make an X and then take a longer vertical stitch down through the center, where the stitches intersect. Bravo! A star is born. This style of stitch may snag if the top vertical stitch is longer than, say, $1/4$ inch. To avoid this you can take a tiny stitch in the center to secure it, or work in as a collection of straight stitches: Work your stitches from the outside in, always entering the fabric toward the center of the star (1–2) and exiting at the star's next point (3) in a clockwise (or counterclockwise, if you prefer) fashion. Try the extra stitch so you can see the different results and discover which you like best. (Psst—I like this one the best!).

ERMINE & SMYRNA

Let's compare stitches! As I said earlier, show me three books on embroidery and I'll show you three different instructions telling you how a stitch should be worked. Some books stick to very tight definitions and certain traditions that dictate precisely how long and short stitches appear in relation to one another, which therefore define the stitch. *Zzzzzz.* Have I lost you already? Well, while I love to buck tradition, I certainly don't mean any disrespect. So here are a couple of stitches that show just what these distinctions can mean. Look at figures 1 and 2. One is an ermine stitch and one is a smyrna stitch. The ermine stitch looks a lot like the twinkle stitch, but one of these things is not like the other. . . . An ermine stitch is worked with the top stitch being the longest, to mimic an ermine tail, or motif. You know, the kind of design you'd see on a royal crest (look up "ermine pattern" online to see what I mean). The smyrna is another one I've found with varying rules. A more traditional smyrna seems to limit itself to a box shape, not allowing any of the extending stitches to be longer than the others. Got it? Okay, enough of the restrictions!

Fern

Fern: Basic

Downward Fern

FERN STITCH

TYPE: *Combination (three straight stitches)*
USED FOR: *Backgrounds, borders, fancy outlining, plant shapes*

THIS IS ONE OF MY FAVORITE STITCHES, which you can probably tell by looking at the projects in the book. It's a beautiful stitch that is fast and easy to work. You can play around with the fern stitch for spectacular, decorative effect, varying the shape of the line and the length of the stitches. This stitch was also a favorite of crazy quilters. It stitches up fast, and covers a lot of ground quickly.

There really is no one way to work this stitch. So, out of the half dozen ways (no kidding) I found this stitch worked from different sources I'm going to give you three versions: the basic method, my downward style, and a cheater's version that works faster and looks just like the real thing. Who knew such a simple little stitch could be so much trouble? Geez! We just want some fern stitches around here!

Basically, a fern stitch is three straight stitches that all converge at the same base point, worked along a central guideline. Notice that to start at the next point (marked X) you'll need to jump a space ahead because your needle can't exit the same entry point last taken. Which also means that this stitch can be worked numerous alternate ways. This stitch is most often worked downward along a vertical line with all the stitches meeting at the base, like a sinuous plant vining up to the sky. This stitch also works beautifully for the center of feathers and leaves. When worked along lines fanning outward from a central point, you have yourself a perfect peacock's tail. Very pretty.

DOWNWARD FERN

More often, I prefer to work a fern stitch with the converging stitches meeting at the top, fanning down, creating a willowy-looking tendril. Clusters of these make wonderful backgrounds of organic shapes and foliage, especially when they cross over and intersect one another. While working downward on a vertical line, the converging stitches will meet at the top of each trio, instead of the bottom. Again, this diagram shows the sequence my stitches naturally take when working like this, but you may find yourself using a different approach to get the same effect. It's the rhythm and repetition you find on your own that will be your preference.

Lazy Fern

LAZY FERN

Psst. Buddy. Wanna know a lazy way to work that fern stitch? Lemme show you what the cool kids do, and no one will be the wiser. Similar to a fly stitch (which is usually isolated like little flies buzzing around, instead of worked along a line in sequence), this lazy fern will mimic the other technique with almost identical results. Take your first stitch (1–2), and come up at 3. Instead of entering the fabric at the base as you normally would, enter across from 3 at 4, but don't pull all the way through just yet—leave some excess floss and keep it looped under the tip of your needle. Now bring your needle out at the base point 5 (same hole as 2) and tug your floss up under your needle as you pull the needle completely through, so it will be tacked down by your next stitch. If you work this by stabbing, your needle will come up at 5, inside the loop of floss, making the downward V. If you work this by sewing, as the diagram shows, you'll use your non-needle hand to pull the floss up under the exiting needle, shaping the V before pulling your needle all the way through. Try it, and see how much it looks like the traditional method for working a fern stitch. I won't tell on you.

Traveling Stitches

HEY LITTLE STITCH, WHERE ARE YOU HEADED? A traveling stitch is one that makes a jump to a new spot when exiting your fabric (like starting a new point in your design, away from the last area you worked), leaving a trail of floss behind it on the backside of your fabric. This is also called a jump stitch. Seasoned needleworkers often like to avoid any traveling stitches and take care while working a stitch to only go where a previous stitch has gone before, following in its footsteps. Why? Well, if your fabric is light, the line of the jump stitch may show through the front of your fabric, depending on how dense or dark it is. I'm a grave sinner of jump stitches and knots. I simply am not that fussy about the backside of my work, unless it is very transparent, or a piece that will need to be ironed (which is when knots and lumps make themselves known on the front side). Many needleworkers have told me over the years that they have been discouraged to take up stitching by being expected to create a backside "as beautiful as the front." That's a pretty tall order to meet, and shouldn't be a standard that gets in the way of learning, having fun, and enjoying embroidery. But, if you'd like to hide where your needle has traveled, simply follow in the footsteps of your last stitch. And if you're not that bothered, don't worry about it. Perfection is to be admired and appreciated, but it's not a requirement for working in embroidery. The only requirement around here is that you enjoy your stitching.

Satin Stitch

Satin Stitch: Stabbing Technique

Satin Padded

Satin Outline

Satin Inline

⦀ SATIN STITCH

TYPE: *Filling / laid*
USED FOR: *Covering an area with solidly worked stitches*

WHEN YOU WANT TO FILL in an area with solid lines, call upon your friend the satin stitch. Of course, you can use any stitch you choose to fill in an area, but this is the quickest way and it gives a variation of texture from the other stitches. The shape of the area you are filling will determine the length of each stitch, and your stitches may be quite long.

After making a stitch, don't exit next to where you just entered (2). Come up across from the last stitch (3), otherwise, you'll just get frustrated trying to make your stitches look close together and having only a few fibers to separate them. In other words, the back of your fabric will look the same as the front. Run your stitches diagonally, vertically, or horizontally across the space you are filling. Whatever floats your boat. Why is it called "satin stitch"? When all those nice, long stitches are finished side by side, they gleam with a satiny sheen.

SATIN PADDED

If you'd like to add some extra pop to your satin stitch to make it really stand up from the fabric, you can pad it first with randomly placed straight stitches. Simply work straight stitches in random fashion (this is also called "seeding") over the area you will cover. Then work your satin stitches over them.

SATIN OUTLINE

It can be tricky to get the edge of a shape worked in satin stitches to look nice and even. If you want to put a finishing touch on an area worked in satin stitches, try outlining the shape with back stitches or split stitches (a different color will highlight the area nicely). It will be easier to do this after you've already worked your satin stitches, and not before—otherwise the tip of the needle might catch on the outlining stitches, which would be irksome.

SATIN INLINE

Another technique for giving an area extra depth is to first outline the shape in back or split stitches, and then work the satin stitches over the outline so the worked stitches are within the edge of the shape, to make the border pop up from your ground fabric.

Traditional Chain: Sewing Technique

Plain Chain: Stabbing Technique

CHAIN STITCHES

CHAIN STITCHES ARE A CATEGORY ALL THEIR OWN. They can be used for outlining, borders, or filling, or to create flowers and raindrops or dangly jewels or dewdrops. . . . A chain stitch can be adapted to numerous variations creating countless effects, which makes it a good one to keep in your bag of stitchy tricks. It's not the fastest stitch to work (which is why I like split stitch so much: it works fast and looks like a tiny chain stitch), but the versatility of chain stitches will give you many other options to play around with.

TRADITIONAL CHAIN: SEWING TECHNIQUE

A traditional chain stitch will have both points exiting from inside the previous loop, or link, in the chain. The sewing technique works most easily for this, and you will need your ground fabric to be loose enough on your hoop (if using one) to be pushed up with your fingers, allowing the needle to make its simultaneous sewing-style entry and exit. Your stitches can be worked in any direction that feels comfortable to you, but I'm going to show this working downward along a vertical line. Come up at 1 and enter the fabric just next to or at the same point (2), without completely pulling your floss all the way through (leave excess floss). Now come up at 3, a small distance along your line (this will determine how long your "link" is). Go ahead and pull the floss until it stops. See how it makes the first link? Next reinsert your needle at the same point as 3 (or just next to it), inside the link (4), and bring the tip of your needle out at 5. Stop! Don't pull your needle all the way through, but while it's in the same position as shown in the diagram, wrap your floss under the needle, making the next link (indicated by the dashed arrow). Now you can pull your needle all the way through, and ta daa! You are chain stitching. Note: make sure that you don't twist the loop before completing each link. (I mean, you can if you want to, but then you're working what's called a twisted chain. Just so ya know.) Finish by securing the last link with a small stitch.

PLAIN CHAIN: STABBING TECHNIQUE

This is how I learned the chain stitch from my mother, who taught me a way that is not the traditional method (my very first lesson in embroidery was already bucking tradition—cool!). This is the stabbing method for chain stitch

Blanket

Buttonhole

Blanket: Traditional

Blanket: Surface

▦ BLANKET (VS. BUTTONHOLE)

THIS IS ONE OF THOSE STITCHES that will make you feel a wee bit smarter (or, just me?) for understanding how to do it. It seems confusing at first, but then you see how simple it really is. It can be worked as a stitch along an edge or on the surface of your fabric.

Many resources use the terms "blanket" and "buttonhole" interchangeably. This is probably because both are worked the same way. However, there actually is a difference to acknowledge: a blanket stitch is open (there are openings between the starting points of each stitch), and the buttonhole is closed (the stitches are worked right up next to each other, finishing the opening for a buttonhole).

Blanket stitches are another playful stitch that you can easily modify and add to by varying the spacing or length of your stitches and interspersing them with other stitches.

TRADITIONAL BLANKET

Look familiar? We've all seen this stitch worked along the edge of a wool throw blanket, giving it a homey touch. Here's how it's done. Bring your needle up from behind the fabric's edge, at the outer tip of the corner. This is a good time to use a tail rather than a knot, so leave excess floss to weave and finish later. Re-insert your needle above and to the right of where your floss exited (2). Keeping the tip of the needle under the fabric's edge, and the excess floss also under the needle as it passes (important!), pull the needle all the way through. By keeping the needle on top of the excess floss, it holds the floss in place, causing it to trail behind, along the edge of the fabric. Repeat.

SURFACE BLANKET

You can also work this as a surface stitch, exactly as above (keeping your needle on top of the fabric), or you can do it the simple, lazy way. I say it's okay. Just take a diagonal stitch (1–2) and when you come up at 3, pull the previous stitch down at a right angle and repeat along your pattern line. Looks exactly the same, and is a good cheat for you stabbing stitchers out there, like me.

Curved Blanket

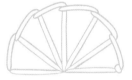

Blanket: Fan

CURVED AND FAN BLANKET

A blanket stitch looks especially pretty along the edge of scalloped fabrics. Don't have a scalloped edge? Fake it! If you work a curvy line above a straight edge of fabric, no one will pay any attention to the straight edge; all eyes'll be on your pretty, curvy blanket stitches.

Let's get crazy. And by "crazy" I mean like crazy quilters. Now that you know how to work a basic blanket stitch, let's turn it on its head and make a fan. This one starts off a little funny, so I'll walk you through it. Exit the fabric at 1 and enter at 2, making a single, long stitch. You'll be returning to the base point at 2 with each following stitch, entering in the same opening. Here's where it seems odd, because you're going to repeat what you just did in the same spots. Come up again at the same point as 1 (3) and return again to the same point as 2 (4). But hold up! Leave excess floss, and now come up inside the excess floss at 5. Return your needle to the base of the fan, and repeat. When you reach the end, secure with a small stitch. To give it even more of an appearance of a fan, add a few straight stitches to the central meeting point like dangly tassels.

It can also be tricky creating a fan of even shape without guide marks that won't end up lopsided (like mine did). The sampler pattern includes an iron-on template you can use for evenly spacing out your stitches and making this fan. You're welcome.

Open Cretan

Open Cretan: Step 1

Open Cretan: Step 2

OPEN CRETAN STITCH

USED FOR: *Borders*

I'M NOT GOING TO LIE TO YOU. This stitch took me a very long time to understand when I first learned it. But it was worth it, because it has a really unique, zig-zag feel. The secret is in the placement of the entry and exit points and how they line up to one another. That wasn't so obvious to me every time I looked it up, until I worked it several times over. Phew!

This is one diagram I ask that you study before you stitch it. Stare intently at it (but keep reading). I want you to notice that 3 exits directly above 2, vertically. See that? That's important. Okay, now I want you to note the horizontal position of 5's exit point to 3 (not the position of the numbers themselves, but where those stitches exit). The exit point for 5 is above the exit point for 3, and not directly across from it. See that? This gives an upward peak for that stitch. The next one will appear horizontally below, giving a downward peak. Another way of looking at this diagram: if you are familiar with the feather stitch, turn the diagram 90 degrees clockwise. See? This is very much like a feather stitch with more deliberate, along-the-lines placement. Now, get your needle and floss ready—go over these instructions again with hoop in hand. I bet it will make better sense to you than it did me.

Way ahead of me there? Wanna sew it? Okay, here's the open Cretan stitch working with the sewing technique. Notice how the floss is kept under your needle. To continue, your needle will work from the other direction. Most books don't include this continuing step, which left me with the impression that you worked the first diagram over and over for this effect. Hey, I'm just a little slow on the uptake, okay?

French Knot

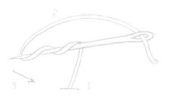

French Knot: Steps 1–3

French Knot: Step 4

⦚ FRENCH KNOT

USED FOR: *Powdering, filling, accents, buds, flower centers*

DON'T BE FOOLED. French knots are really easy—the trick is in explaining the technique. But once you get the hang of it, you'll want French knots sprinkled everywhere. This is my favorite decorative stitch. It's fun to do and makes for a nice detail that fills up an area quickly. How? Like this.

STEP 1: Pull the floss up through the fabric and hold it taut (1). Now, set the hoop in your lap or on your working surface, as you will be using both hands for the next steps.

STEP 2: Pinch the floss—say, half of its length—using the hand not holding the needle. Keep it taut.

STEP 3: Wind the floss that's between your pinched fingers and the fabric once or twice around the needle (2). For ease, keep your needle in front of the floss and wind the floss in a counterclockwise motion toward you. Wind once for a small knot or twice for a bigger one. Three times if your floss is very fine. But you don't want to keep on winding it—then it becomes a bullion.

STEP 4: With the strands wound tightly along your needle (don't let them go loose), partially reinsert the needle just next to where it exited the fabric (1), but (here's the most important step!) before you push the needle through, pull the floss you've been holding with your non-needle hand so the tightly wound strands slide down the needle and make a little bundle against the fabric (4). Now push your needle completely through to finish. Voilà!

    Whenever you see a little circle on a pattern, it typically indicates a French knot. Dot the ends of vines with these to make little flower buds, or use them here and there for a little nubby texture.

Herringbone

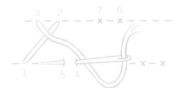

Sewing Technique

⬛ HERRINGBONE

USED FOR: *Borders*

THIS IS A TYPE OF CROSS-STITCH that works most easily with the sewing method. If you work it in the sewing method, you'll only be able to work it in one color of thread. Or, you can work it like a standard cross-stitch with the stabbing technique (one pass of diagonal stitches, then a second pass) with the same look, and take advantage of introducing a new color of thread with your second pass of stitches. Also, my illustration shows the crossed areas being really tiny, but yours don't have to be. Look at the sewing diagram for example, where the ends are wider apart (3–2). See? We're not overly concerned about that; it's an aesthetic decision, all up to you.

To make this stitch, you'll follow along imaginary or visible guidelines. Come up at 1, and then enter and exit the fabric simultaneously at 2 and 3. Your next stitch will enter and exit at 4 and 5. Notice your needle is working in the opposite direction (pulling to the left) while your stitches advance in the other direction.

Sheaf Stitch

▦ SHEAF STITCH

USED FOR: *Powdering, accents*

TAKE THREE LONG STITCHES and then bring them together with a small straight stitch, beginning inside the outer stitches, pulling them inward, for a tidy decorative sheaf (see the project on page 94).

▦ LEAF STITCH

HERE'S ANOTHER CROSS-STITCH VARIATION that's easy to work. It's called a leaf stitch because (isn't it obvious?) it works perfectly to illustrate the veins of a leaf. The dashed outline on my diagram is there just as an example of a leaf-shaped pattern and how you might place the stitches within that shape. You could also use this stitch to represent a plant, by topping it off with a lazy daisy and putting some French knots at the tip of each outward extending stitch. Say, that sounds like combining stitches. Why, yes, it is! You can do very interesting things by combining stitches, so I've included a section on stitch combinations just for you.

Leaf Stitch

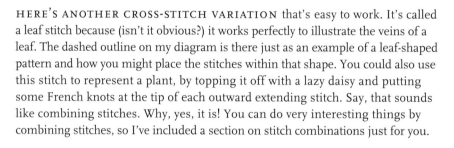

There are also . . .

STITCH COMBINATIONS

LITTLE RECIPES MADE UP OF STITCHES

Sweet · Pretty · Gorgeous

Stitch combinations are like little recipes made up of stitches you can use without necessarily following a pattern. Sometimes the most seemingly complex arrangements of stitches are just artful combinations made up of simple stitches we already know. That's why increasing your repertoire of stitches will give you endless possibilities of combinations and more versatility. As you get comfortable with more stitches, you'll find you can quickly construct little motifs in embroidery: a fern stitch dotted with French knots makes a quick and easy budding vine.

MANY DECORATIVE COMBINATIONS WERE SPAWNED BY THE CRAZY-QUILTING FAD. Quilting is almost a misnomer here, because this Victorian hobby didn't involve any actual quilting—it was all about the crazy, elaborate embroidery stitches covering a patchwork blanket of silks, satins, and velvets. Embroidery stitches in repeated combinations were used heavily all over, creating jaw-dropping displays of embellishment.

Here are some stitch combinations inspired by crazy quilts as well as some new combos I created for you to try. I'm sure you'll see other ways you can add to and embellish these combos as you work with them, which is precisely the idea! Again, this is just a teeny tiny sampling of possible combos to get you thinking, and starting points for building your own. Check the resources sections where I've listed some books that are nothing but stitch combinations of endless varieties!

CROSS + FRENCH KNOTS AND CROSS + HIDDEN

Let's start with two very simple combos that make a quick and easy border. For each, work your cross-stitches first, then you'll take a second pass in French knots or the hidden stitch (try a different color!). For the hidden stitch, include a stitch that passes over the center of each X.

Cross + French Knots   *Cross + Hidden*

OPEN CRETAN STACKED + FRENCH KNOTS

Stagger two rows of open Cretan stitches and accent every other outward point with a French knot. Easy to do, and looks mighty impressive!

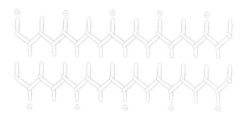

LAZY LOTUS + {BRICK} RIPPLE

Work the ripple stitch in two different shades of blue along a wavy line. Decorate each curve with a lotus, alternating sides, and you have lovely blooms in a rippling stream.

SHEAF + FRENCH KNOTS + HIDDEN

The sheaf stitch is so quick and easy to work to great effect. Just dot the ends with another color of French knots, intersperse each sheaf with cross-stitches, and finish with hidden stitches to create a dramatic border.

STEM + STRAIGHT + FRENCH KNOTS + CROSS

It's just so easy to make flowers from stitches. Some simple stems, some straight stitches (or lazy daisy) for quick petals, French knots at the tips, and some upward shoots of greenery make it all too easy. A little X appears in between repeats of the pattern for an extra bit of color.

BLANKET {FAN} + FRENCH KNOTS + STRAIGHT

Ooh, look what you can do with that curved blanket stitch as a fan! Alternate up and down and add straight stitches and French knots for a playful row of dancing, tasseled fans!

HERRINGBONE + HIDDEN + FRENCH KNOTS + LAZY DAISY

This is a modified herringbone stitch (notice how every other one "disappears"?). Work these stitches first and then pass over with a hidden stitch (again, grab a new color!). Top off with a few lazy daisies. I can already hear you thinking of new things you can do with this . . .

BLANKET {CURVED} + FRENCH KNOTS + LAZY DAISY {SURFACE STITCH}

I think this combination looks like a candelabra, don't you? If working a curved blanket stitch along an edge, of course you'll have to leave those lazy daisy stitches off. But this combo can be worked just as easily as a surface blanket stitch, which means you can add those extra stitches below the design (version shown).

And finally . . .

EXTRA EFFECTS

WOW YOUR FRIENDS AND LOVED ONES

◇◇◇◇◇◇◇◇◇◇◇◇◇◇◇◇◇◇◇◇◇◇◇◇◇◇◇

Sequins · Beads · Things that Glow

◇◇◇

Want to do something a little unusual with your stitches, or embellish them even more? Here are three easy, but impressive, ways you can make sure your needlework commands admiring attention.

◇◇◇◇

SEQUINS AND BEADS

THE GLITTER OF NEEDLEWORK! Used sparingly or with unrestrained abandon, sequins can add an extra "ooh" to your projects. I can't resist sprinkling them here and there after a project is all stitched up. My favorites are the clear kind with an iridescent shimmer. Clear sequins are more subtle than silver ones (if subtle is what you're going for), showing only their shine instead of themselves. But I have nothing against liberal use of sequins. What constitutes "too many sequins" will be left entirely up to you.

There are a few different ways you can attach sequins. You can sew them in place, or secure them with a bead (in which case you'll need a beading needle). In either case, you'll need a slimmer needle and you'll want to use thread (or you can improvise with a single strand of floss). You may want to match the color of your thread to the sequin, or not. Up to you. I like to apply sequins individually, as opposed to stranding them all in a row (which covers half of the last sequin preceding it). You can also get pre-banded ribbons of sequins if you really want to go whole hog with them.

To attach a sequin: come up through the center of the sequin (you'll know immediately if your needle is too big or not), and take a stitch down, securing it. Come up again through the center, and down again across from the previous stitch (like nine and three o'clock). That's it!

Important! Do not pass a hot iron directly over your sequins. They will lose their shine and, at worst, shrivel up and die. If they do, you can remove them and replace with new ones—but let's avoid having to do that in the first place, hokay?

Sequin Tips

◇◇◇◇◇◇◇◇◇◇◇◇◇◇◇◇◇◇◇◇◇

SOME OF THE TRANSFER PATTERNS in this book have spots designated for placement of sequins. Wherever you see a circle with a dot in the middle, it means "a sequin goes here"! Don't wanna put a sequin there? That's cool—just stitch around or over the little circle on the pattern.

◇◇◇◇◇◇◇◇◇◇◇◇◇◇◇◇◇◇◇◇◇

FOR SPARKLE THAT CATCHES THE ADMIRER BY SURPRISE, use sequins of a color that matches the fabric they're applied to: red sequins on red fabric, black sequins on black fabric.

GLOW-IN-THE-DARK THREAD

WILL WONDERS NEVER CEASE? Finally companies are starting to develop glow-in-the-dark threads in a wide range of colors. The biggest selection of colors comes in fine braids instead of stranded floss (which is available in only one color), meaning that you won't be able to divide the strands down or split them. No biggie—you can still stitch with them!

While using nothing but glow-in-the-dark threads to stitch up an entire pattern is dramatic, I like the sneaky touch. How about stitching up a design with traditional threads that slyly interweaves glowing threads as accents on the pattern? Others will surely notice your needlework light up when the sun goes down.

FLOSS BLENDING

THINK OF THIS AS MIXING PAINT. You'll need stranded floss for this technique. Take a few strands of one color and a few strands from another. For best results strip the strands so they are even with one another, or you may have snagging occur. Thread both colors on your needle and stitch! You'll get an ice-cream swirl mix with your stitches. This creates an optical illusion, too: if you're mixing certain colors (like blue and yellow) the viewer's eye may perceive it as green from a distance. Neato.

INSPIRED? ITCHING TO GET STITCHING?

This is the best part! Once you've caught the embroidery bug, nothing will be safe from your stitches. All of the projects in this book combine the techniques we've covered up to this point, so there should be no major surprises. Each project makes use of a transfer design included at the back of this book, or creatively combines stitches and techniques you've just learned—no transfer needed. And the best part: none of these projects are strictly by-the-number, do-this and then do-that cookie-cutter projects. They leave plenty of room to become your own, truly personal works by hand. Some projects are very simple and can be finished in an evening, while other projects will allow you to work over time and can be as simple or detailed as you make them.

Blank, finished (meaning: ready-to-use) textiles are the most tempting for our stitches—on a readymade apron, tablecloth, shirt, skirt, or pillowcase. This isn't a sewing book, so I've mostly tried to leave out projects that require sewing. I'm sure you'll find plenty of things on hand that you'll want to stitch. I've also provided information in the resources guide for finding the same textiles used for many of the projects in this book.

And hey—don't be intimidated about expanding your embroidery or stitching outside the lines. Embroidery can look so intricate and complicated, but you can do it, and you can do whatever you want with it. The most important thing is to have fun and enjoy your stitching.

BIG OL' TRANSFERS

A NOTE ON THE TRANSFERS: some of the transfers included in this book are of a larger format and will require extra care when ironing on to fabric. You will be ironing a large area, which means a greater likelihood of shifting the pattern and leaving a ghostly, misplaced transfer. You might want to pin or tape down larger transfers, and be sure to iron the entire transfer evenly to avoid any blank spots.

THE SCALE:

Not every pattern in this book is suited to every stitcher. I've broken it down for you here, and you'll see these icons on the tabs that label each project. Think of this as just another way to avoid unnecessary tears and frustration.

🎩 = **BEGINNERS,** *or those after something quick & fun.*

🎩🎩 = **INTERMEDIATE,** *or a bit of experience needed.*

🎩🎩🎩 = **ADVANCED,** *challenging but worth it!*

Palette

IN CASE YOU'D LIKE TO MATCH the colors of floss shown on each project, here's a list of color numbers so you can work within the palette I used. There may be slight variations in hues from what the photos show, and extra colors may appear here and there, but this list of floss colors covers the spectrum stitched on the projects. The numbers given here are for Presencia brand floss, which you can easily order online (see Resources, page 149), if not available from your local needlework shop. They also offer a conversion chart for color numbers to correspond with DMC and Anchor brand floss, if that is your preference (or what you already have on hand).

Of course, choosing your own favorite floss colors is the most fun, so don't feel you have to re-create these projects down to the last, perfectly matched shade (or stitch)! They're shown for your inspiration and guidance.

I've grouped like colors together (grays, blues, etc.) and have listed them from lightest to darkest. I've also given the manufacturer's color name for each, but will use a more general color name when referencing them with the project in case you'd like to easily pick out colors without having to track numbers.

Build your palette with:

8683 Very Light Pearl Gray
8688 Pearl Gray
8705 Steel Gray

1724 Light Pale Geranium
2323 Cyclamen Pink
2333 Dark Cyclamen Pink
1166 Bright Red
1984 Medium Antique Rose

1325 Tangerine

1134 Light Pale Yellow
1010 Medium Straw
1232 Deep Canary

1000 Blanc
3000 Ecru

3639 Very Light Teal
3476 Dark Bay Blue
3822 Dark Electric Blue

4550 Yellow Green
4636 Chartreuse

2606 Pale Violet
2615 Violet

HOME

Feather your nest with

STIT

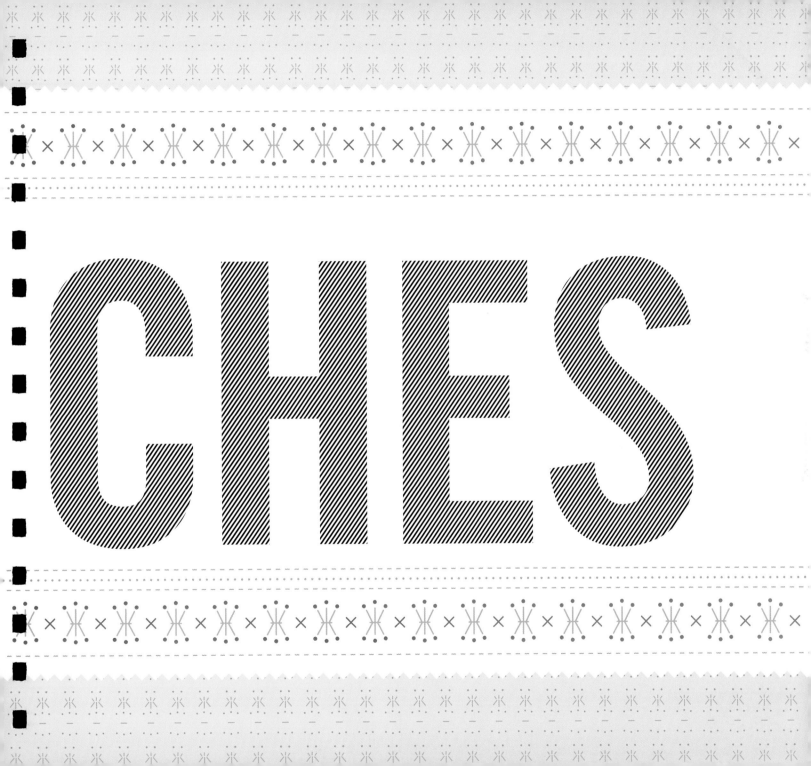

Stitch SAMPLER

NEED A STARTING PROJECT? Here's a completely painless one designed to help you learn nearly all of the stitches I've reviewed (sheaf and satin are not included). Samplers are a very old tradition for learning new stitches and showing off your skills. Here's a not-so-old-looking sampler for you to practice on. Yes, it looks intimidating as a finished project, but approach it as practice and you'll be just fine. Remember you, can use the transfer more than once. So, have at it!

You can transfer the entire sheet to a piece of doodle fabric for framing (careful not to shift it while ironing), or transfer the design to a finished textile like a square zippered pillow cover (see Resources, page 150). I've left the diagram numbers off the sampler transfer so you'll have a finished version you can proudly display. Instead, see the illustrated legend below for guidance (it will decipher the dots for you). But remember: this is your practice sampler, so it's okay if it ends up only being a place to play and practice your stitches.

Some notes on my sampler in case you're curious: I gently tacked down the threaded border with a single strand of the same color floss in the center of those outwardly curving stitches, and used two different grays for the cross-stitches in 3 ply. I used a pale green floss and a bright green floss blended together to work the fern stitches. Hidden stitches were worked along the row of herringbone where they cross, and stitched in another color. For the leaf shapes, I stitched the outline first before working the inner leaf stitch. Extend your leaf stitch beyond the outline of the leaf shape, in a different green. See what I mean? Mmmhmm. Of course, you could always do something different . . .

STITCHES & SUPPLIES

TEXTILE:
Plain cotton scrap

PATTERN:
See transfers section for "Stitches I Know" template. See page 154 for stitch map.

STITCHES USED:
threaded backstitch (with tacked stitches) (page 54)
open brick (page 56)
cross (page 57)
open cretan (page 67)
herringbone (page 69)
lazy daisy (page 63)
lazy lotus (page 64)
French knot (page 68)
blanket: surface (page 65)
blanket: fan (page 66)
back (page 54)
leaf (page 70)
fern (page 59)
twinkle (page 58)
plain chain (linked) (page 62)
magic chain (page 64)
scalloping chain (page 64)

COLORS USED:
All of them!

TECHNIQUES AND EFFECTS:
Silver and gold metallic thread (see Resources, page 150)
Blended floss (fern stitch).

EXTRA SUPPLIES AND TOOLS:
The sampler is shown on an 11" x 11" square Q-Snap frame (see Resources, page 149).

Mahjong TABLECLOTH

MORE EXOTIC THAN BRIDGE and more colorful than dominoes, the Chinese tile game of mahjong (no, not the one on your computer) is my other favorite way to unwind. The chunky game tiles have such pretty images on them, making perfect motifs for embroidery. Instead of hearts, clubs, and spades, mahjong has winds, flowers, and birds. I positioned the design on the tablecloth to sit along the edge of the tabletop instead of below the table's edge so it can be admired by the players. Mahjong!

STITCHES & SUPPLIES

TEXTILE:
See Resources (page 150)
for tablecloth.

PATTERN:
See transfer section for
"Mahjong" template.

STITCHES USED:
open brick (page 56)
back (page 54)
lazy lotus (page 64)
herringbone (page 69)

COLORS USED:
1166 red
3639 pale blue
4636 bright green
1010 medium yellow
1724 pale pink
8705 dark gray
8683 pale gray

TECHNIQUES AND EFFECTS:
Sequins (page 80)

MAH JONG

Fan Dancer SHOWER CURTAIN

ADD SOME SHOWTIME TO YOUR SHOWER! Large, feathery fans are a great excuse for using the fern stitch. (Obviously we're stitching on a cotton curtain here, and not a plastic one.) Don't be intimidated by its size. With the transfer from the back of the book of the fan dancer, the design alternates with the sheaf combination (see page 75) placed horizontally along the lower third of the curtain. (Kind stitcher, please note: the project example here uses individual straight stitches on the sheaf design as an alternative to long stitches bundled together.) Hidden stitches alternated with blanket stitches create a border finishing off the edge. When working on a large textile like this (which probably isn't very often), blanket stitches and border combos will allow you to cover a lot of ground quickly to lend a finished look.

Faces can be hard to re-create in embroidery. I've tried to make the design as simple as possible, so you can execute the eyes, nose, and mouth in a few deft stitches. Just follow the lines and strip your floss down to two or three plys to maintain detail. Her eyes are French knots (what else?) worked in three-ply, wound twice around the needle.

STITCHES & SUPPLIES

TEXTILE:
See Resources (page 150) for shower curtain.

PATTERN:
See transfer section for "Fan Dancer" template, "sheaf stitch" template (found with sugar skulls), and "blanket fan" template (found on sampler).

STITCHES USED:
stem (page 53)
split (page 52)
fern (page 59)
sheaf (page 70)
blanket: basic (page 65)
blanket: fan (page 66)
cross (page 57)
hidden (page 55)
French knot (page 68)

COLORS USED:
2323 medium pink
2333 dark pink
1134 pale yellow
1325 orange
1724 pale pink

TECHNIQUES AND EFFECTS:
Sequins (page 80)

"Born to Stitch" THROW PILLOW

THIS IS A PILLOW I MADE FOR MYSELF, but couldn't resist sharing as a project for you, too. I really had fun with this project, making use of all of my favorite stitches, experimenting with colors and using whatever stitch I wanted wherever I felt like it. Because the size of the transfer sheet only has room for the central design shown here, you can personalize it with your own emblems and favorite stitches. Heck, you might even want to change up the message to say "Stitched by Moi" or "Born to be Crewel." And . . . how would you do that?

Lettering can pose an (easily beatable) challenge when you want to craft your own quote. Transfer alphabets can be difficult to cut and piece together—but most of us have printers so conveniently available! Simply type up your wise (or snarky) words in a typeface you enjoy and print it out for your own pattern, using a transfer method of your choice (see page 38). After all, who am I to tell you what to say?

STITCHES & SUPPLIES

TEXTILE:
See Resources (page 150) for zippered pillow case.

PATTERN:
See transfer section for "Born to Stitch" (central design) template.

STITCHES USED:
split (page 52)
back (page 54)
satin (page 61)
twinkle (page 58)
fern (page 59)
hidden (page 55)
stem (page 53)
lazy daisy (page 63)

plain chain (page 62)
traditional chain (page 62)
cross (page 57)
French knot (page 68)

COLORS USED:
The whole palette!

TECHNIQUES AND EFFECTS:
I alternated colors of the petals on one of the lazy daisies, which is part of the embellished design. Try it! Skip every other petal when stitching, then re-floss your needle with a different color and complete the other petals.

BORN TO STITCH

Embellished PHOTO PORTRAIT

TRANSFERRING PHOTOS TO FABRIC has been a favorite technique of quilters for years. The down 'n' dirty method was to take a photocopy of a photograph, lay it image-side down on fabric, and rub it with a cotton ball soaked in solvent, burnishing the image into the fibers. The result was a soft, ghostly transfer of the photo, with imperfect edges, now on your fabric. Lovely. However, this method apparently won't work anymore due to improvements made by manufacturers to their toners (making them solvent resistant).

The good news is, it's easier than ever to get photographic images onto fabric with ink-jet and laser printers, without using toxic chemicals and solvents. The bad news is, this is most often with commercially manufactured fabric sheets that you just stick in the printer. They're fine for sewing into another project, like a quilt block, but what if you want the photo on your very own fabric so you can embroider all over it? The plastic-y sheets don't lend themselves well to being stitched on directly. Don't fret, there's still a way to do it, dear. We just have to work around technology's darned improvements a bit. Turn the page for complete instructions.

STITCHES & SUPPLIES

TEXTILE:
Choose a plain weave cotton (not a knit, like a T-shirt).

PATTERN:
I used a photo of my mom from the '60s!

STITCHES USED:
back (page 54)
split (page 52)
French knot (page 68)
open cretan (page 67)
isolated chain (page 63)
straight stitches (no diagram—just single stitches powdering the background)

COLORS USED:
You'll be picking your own colors for your project, but I used more muted tones so as not to overwhelm the faded look of the fabric transfer. Maybe you'll go a different direction with your project, like stitching bold colors on a black-and-white transfer!

TECHNIQUES AND EFFECTS:
I layered quilt batting behind the fabric as a ground to give it a pillowy, quilted look (see page 30) and added sequins.

EXTRA SUPPLIES AND TOOLS:
Foam core and straight pins for mounting. I used a store-bought frame with the glass removed (be sure to read about framing techniques on page 142).

Continued . . .

Scan your image and size it to the dimensions you want. Before I printed my photo, I tried to regain some of the solvent-transfer charm by using a computer graphics program to randomly burn out selected areas of the image (which became the floating "bubbles") using the eraser tool set with a large diameter and soft edges.

As soon as your image is print-ready, cut a piece of fabric and a piece of freezer paper, each to 8.5" x 11" (or any other size that your printer will accommodate and you'd like to work in). It's important that you cut to the same size as a printable sheet—we don't want you to risk jamming your printer. With a hot, dry iron, iron the freezer paper (plastic side) to the fabric. Iron long enough to make sure the corners of each sheet are not peeling away by themselves. Let it cool for just a moment before you put it in the printer (but don't let it sit too long either). If you've never done this before, you'll be giddy when you see your image whirring out of the printer, directly onto your fabric. Peel away the freezer paper backing and discard. Now, with your photo on the fabric, prepare to be brilliant and stitch around and over your image to your heart's content. I worked out parts of my design first, drawing directly on tracing paper by laying it over the photo for positioning, and then re-tracing those lines with carbon transfer paper once I had them where I wanted them.

Glow-in-the-Dark Chandelier MAGNETS

LET'S EMBROIDER YOUR REFRIGERATOR, shall we? For those nights when we find ourselves up and headed for the kitchen, bumping into things, these little chandelier magnets will give a friendly glow. The widest range of colors for glow-in-the-dark threads are available as fine braids (instead of stranded floss). If working with braids, be aware that you will not be able to separate away the strands, or work them as a split stitch. All other stitches are go!

The nice thing about crafting felt is that it's easy-to-stitch, and you don't need a hoop or stabilizer. Choose felts in your favorite colors and be sure to get the stiff felt—not the flimsy fleece. Iron the chandelier design directly onto a pre-cut felt square and stitch. For this project, the glow-in-the-dark threads are used for accenting, not embroidering the entire design (but

you certainly can do it that way). After the design has been stitched, cut around it, leaving an edge about $1/4"$ wide, giving your fingers something to grab whenever you move the magnet. Use a strong craft adhesive (white craft paste or rubber cement won't hold up for this job) like hot glue, and adhere the magnets to the center of the stitched felt's back. You can choose the type of magnet base you want to use: those chunky discs or flat, flexible sheets you can cut close to the shape of the felt outline. Apply even pressure and allow to dry. Enjoy your embroidery design at night.

STITCHES & SUPPLIES

TEXTILE:
Stiff craft felt

PATTERN:
See transfer section for "Chandelier" template.

STITCHES USED:
back (page 54)
French knot (page 68)
twinkle (page 58)

COLORS USED:
(on pink magnet)
2606 pale violet
1724 pale pink
1134 pale yellow

(on blue magnet)
3639 pale blue
3476 gray blue
1134 pale yellow
1000 white
3000 ivory

TECHNIQUES AND EFFECTS:
Glow-in-the-dark threads (see Resources, page 149) for the flames and twinkles.
Sequins (page 80)

EXTRA SUPPLIES AND TOOLS:
Craft magnets
Hot glue gun

"Let Me Sleep" PILLOWCASE

WANT TO SEND A MESSAGE when you're not awake to say it? One of the first just-for-me embroidery projects I made was to embroider these words along the edge of my pillow. What can I say? I'm a light sleeper and don't like to be disturbed when catching my ZZZ's.

Wondering about whether or not to stitch through both layers on the end of your pillowcase? If you are comfortable opening a seam and sewing it back up, it will mean you only have to stitch through one layer of fabric to embroider your project (easier on the digits!) and will also hide the back when you sew it back up, if that's your preference. You also have my full permission to just grab any ol' pillowcase and stitch it up as-is, and not worry your pretty little head about sewing up a thing. (Psst— you can also cheat the design a bit by working it on the area above the doubled end, to give it a decorative border.)

STITCHES & SUPPLIES

TEXTILE:
Standard pillowcase

PATTERN
See transfer section for "Let Me Sleep" template.

STITCHES USED:
hidden (page 55)
stem (page 53)
twinkle (page 58)
plain chain (linked) (page 62)
magic chain (page 64)
scalloping chain (page 64)

COLORS USED:
1000 white
1010 medium yellow
2333 dark pink

TECHNIQUES AND EFFECTS:
When I stitched the lettering, I used a hidden stitch (it's like a whisper!) with the stabbing method instead of the sewing technique to keep the stitches short and neat. To avoid transfer lines appearing in between your stitches, lightly trace this design with carbon transfer paper instead.

Amy Butler Lotus LAPTOP CASE

AMY BUTLER'S GORGEOUS FABRICS have large, decorative motifs that provide a wonderful ground design for combining with decorative embroidery stitches, no pattern needed. Practice your edging, powdering, and outlining on this, and it will look fanciful and beautiful, no matter what.

This is one of the few projects I've included that requires sewing. If you sew, you have the advantage of embroidering your fabric after it has been cut and before it is sewn together—it can be difficult to work on a project after the sewing is done (think tight, narrow sleeve). If enlisting the help of a friend who sews, ask them to let you embroider the pieces after they've been cut, and talk about where you'd like your stitches to appear on the finished case. For this project, we've put stitches only in one area, so they'll be admired when your computer is in tow, and show that there's a little extra something you've added to that already gorgeous fabric.

STITCHES & SUPPLIES

TEXTILE:
Amy Butler fabric in "Lotus"

STITCHES USED:
back (page 54)
traditional blanket (page 65)
sheaf (page 70)
fern (page 59)
traditional chain (page 62)

stem (page 53)
isolated chain (page 63)
French knot (page 68)

COLORS USED:
1134 pale yellow
1010 medium yellow
2323 medium pink
4550 pale green
1984 brownish pink

TECHNIQUES AND EXTRA EFFECTS:
When looking at this fabric pattern, notice how those pink and gray shapes could also be turned into birds by stitching their beaks, eyes, and wings. You may see things in patterned fabrics that you can bring out with embroidery!

EXTRA SUPPLIES AND TOOLS:
Amy Butler Laptop Cover pattern (see Resources, page 150)

Stitched Señorita CARD

WHEN MIXED WITH UNEXPECTED MEDIA, embroidery steals the show. Here's where you can really be creative and bring in your other craft supplies like glitter, endpapers, paints, pens, and pastels. Or, you can embellish an existing found image with playfully incorporated embroidery. Iron-on transfers will also print on heavy papers (and wood), offering you even more options for designs (see page 31 for techniques on how to stitch on paper).

If working with a found image, it might first need to be mounted to stiffer paper for stitching. Here's a foolproof way to get the paper to stick without becoming bubbly or eventually peeling away: take rubber cement (new cement, not gummy old stuff) and apply a thin, even coat to the back of the image and also the surface of the blank card. Allow each to set apart for a full 30 seconds (yes, a *full* 30 seconds) before applying to each other.

When you stick the papers together, they will stick like crazy without any possibility of lifting and re-positioning, so if your image will become the full front of the card, do not cut the pieces first, attempting to match them perfectly at the same time you're gluing them together. Glue first, and trim down after. Burnish the papers together from the center out with the nail of your thumb or a bone folder, and press under a weighted book for a couple of hours. Those papers are not going to come apart now for anyone or anything! After the card has dried, you can prep it with holes for stitching.

To include a written note, choose a colored paper you like and insert it in your card after writing your message, adhering the top and bottom corners of the left-facing fold to the back of the card's front (to hide the backs of your stitches). Hello, penpal.

STITCHES & SUPPLIES

PAPER:
100 lb acid-free Bristol board (available at art and craft supply stores).

PATTERN USED:
Found image of a dancer (see Resources, page 151).

STITCHES USED:
hidden (page 55)
scalloping chain (page 64)
twinkle (page 58)
cross (page 57)
threaded backstitch (page 54)
plain chain (page 62)
back (page 54)
French knot (page 68)
blanket: fan (page 66)
isolated chain (page 63)

COLORS USED:
1000 white
1010 medium yellow
4636 bright green
3476 gray blue
1325 orange

TECHNIQUES AND EXTRA EFFECTS:
Gold and red metallic ribbon (see Resources, page 150).

EXTRA SUPPLIES AND TOOLS:
Rubber cement

Childish INSPIRATION

FOR DECADES (AND SURELY LONGER), needle-workers have turned to children's drawings as designs for embroidery. What collaboration could be sweeter? Not just for adults, this is also a wonderful way to get children stitching with their own creations.

This is a portrait of me drawn by my ten-year-old niece. I used long, un-fussy stitches to follow her lines to mimic the freedom of the drawing. Often we pay such close attention to the neatness and precision of our grown-up stitches, but it can be just as rewarding to be inspired by the free-form lines of a child.

STITCHES & SUPPLIES

TEXTILE:
Plain weave cotton

STITCHES USED:
back (page 54)
stem (page 53)
straight (no diagram—
just single stitches)
herringbone (page 69)
French knot (page 68)
satin (page 61)
isolated chain (page 63)

COLORS USED:
You'll want to choose your own colors for your child's drawing, maybe matching the colors he or she used.

TECHNIQUES AND EXTRA EFFECTS:
Sequins (page 80)
Carbon Papers (page 38)

EXTRA SUPPLIES AND TOOLS:
Foam core and straight pins for mounting. I used a store-bought frame with the glass removed (be sure to read about framing techniques on (page 142).

Felt Flower BOUQUET

LET'S TAKE FELT FLOWERS FURTHER. The cut-felt flower is one of my favorite craft projects. Sweet, simple, and no two could ever be alike. But instead of just adorning ourselves with solitary blooms on our lapels, let's create a bouquet, with never-fading embroidery stitches embellishing the petals.

Cut, free-hand, flowers in any shape you like. It will be up to you if you want to embroider your flowers before or after you cut them. It will be easier to work your stitches on uncut shapes, but take extreme care not to accidentally snip your embroidery when cutting them out. (Of course, whipped and blanket stitches along the edge can be worked only after the shapes are cut.)

To make a stemmed flower and start building a bouquet, take a piece of floral wire and crimp it back on itself at one end (about one half an inch or longer). Poke two holes about an eighth of an inch apart with your needle (should be a smaller gauge needle than the wire) through the center of the base pieces of your flower (set aside the center piece). Then pass the floral wire through the front of the flower in one hole until you reach the crimped end, and then guide the bent wire end through the second hole. Push the wire all the way against the felt, and pinch the wire against itself on the underside. Now, attach the center piece with tiny stitches in one strand of floss. Just a few should do the trick. Place the leaf shapes along the wire stem either together or apart. Ahh, a bouquet of stitches that will never wilt.

STITCHES & SUPPLIES

TEXTILE:
Stiff craft felt

STITCHES USED:
isolated chain (page 63)
leaf (page 70)
French knot (page 68)
back (page 54)
cross (page 57)
hidden (page 55)
blanket: fan (page 66)

COLORS USED:
2606 pale violet
3000 ivory
2333 dark pink
1724 pale pink
1010 medium yellow
3476 gray blue
1984 brownish pink

TECHNIQUES AND EXTRA EFFECTS:
Sequins (page 80)

EXTRA SUPPLIES AND TOOLS:
20-gauge floral stem wire,
florist foam (available at large craft stores)

FASHION

◇◇◇◇◇◇◇◇◇◇◇◇◇◇◇◇◇◇◇◇◇◇◇◇◇

Everyone looks better in

EMBR

Funky Sashiko KIMONO

SASHIKO IS A TYPE OF TRADITIONAL JAPANESE embroidery that is worked entirely in stitches of only one color thread, with very simple designs often echoing forms found in nature, such as clouds, fish scales, or foliage. Traditionally sashiko is worked with great precision, with every hidden stitch being uniform in length and spacing. Only appearing difficult to do, this is easily achieved by a pattern that defines where your needle enters and exits the fabric. It's also used on humble household textiles and was originally used for quilting layers of fabric together.

I've loosened up one of sashiko's motifs for you and created a repeatable pattern inspired by a traditional sashiko motif of fishing nets. You can take the transfer from this book and repeat it end-to-end to make the pattern your desired length.

STITCHES & SUPPLIES

TEXTILE:
See Resources (page 150) for satin kimono.

PATTERN USED:
See transfer section for "Funky Sashiko" template.

STITCHES USED:
hidden (page 55)

COLOR USED:
3000 ivory

TECHNIQUES AND EXTRA EFFECTS:
Stabilizers (page 34)
Carbon Papers (page 38)

Tattoo Heart ON YOUR SLEEVE

EMBROIDERY AND TATTOOS: the *perfect* marriage of needle arts! What better place to stitch up a tattoo than on your sleeve? Combining tattoo designs with needlework has been one of my favorite ways to update embroidery, and who doesn't love the look of a classy, vintage tattoo? This is one you can take off at the end of the day though (to show off your real ones).

This project will take some very, very simple sewing. To make life easier, I opened up the seam of the sleeve to the armpit, allowing easier access to the back of the fabric. After you finish stitching this bad boy up, turn that shirt inside out, and machine sew the seam up again (or enlist the help of a sewing friend). Nice work you got there.

STITCHES & SUPPLIES

TEXTILE:
See Resources (page150)
for work shirt.

PATTERN USED:
See transfer section for
"Tattoo" template.

STITCHES USED:
back (page 54)
stem (page 53)
fern (page 59)
satin (page 61)
French knot (page 68)
hidden (page 55)
lazy daisy (page 63)
cross (page 57)
straight stitches (no diagram—
just single stitches)

COLORS USED:
8688 medium gray
1166 red
1010 medium yellow
1134 pale yellow
1325 orange
2333 dark pink
3822 bright blue

Peacock Bomber JACKET

LET'S STITCH OUR OWN satin souvenir jacket (instead of waiting forever to luck out and find the right one). Bomber jackets just never go out of style, and can be easily scored new or as vintage wear. This jacket is satin, but you might also deck one out that's cotton. Nothing says you can't stitch this jacket in phases, either, wearing it and embroidering it bit by bit . . . let your design build and grow into an impressive work of stitchery.

STITCHES & SUPPLIES

TEXTILE:
Hunt re-sale stores or online for a good bomber jacket! It doesn't have to be satin.

PATTERN USED:
See transfer section for "Peacock" template.

STITCHES USED:
back (page 54)
fern (page 59)
stem (page 53)
whipped stem (page 53)
French knot (page 68)
satin (page 61)
cross (page 57)
straight (no diagram—just single stitches)

COLORS USED:
3000 ivory
1232 dark yellow
3639 pale blue
3476 gray blue
8683 pale gray
8705 dark gray
1166 red
2323 medium pink

TECHNIQUES AND EXTRA EFFECTS:
Sequins (page 80).

Mexican Sugar Skulls WRAP SKIRT

DECORATIVELY FROSTED SUGAR SKULLS that abound during the traditional Mexican holiday of Day of the Dead inspire a perfectly delicious design for embroidery. Wrap skirts are wonderfully simple to stitch on because they completely open up flat and are adjustable to one-size-fits-all. Get ready to practice your lazy daisy! Mexican sugar skulls inspire the use of lots of color and small flowers. It's impossible to add too many of them to this design—the more the better.

STITCHES & SUPPLIES

TEXTILE:
See Resources (page 150) for wrap skirt.

PATTERN USED:
See transfer section for "Sugar Skulls" template.

STITCHES USED:
back (page 54)
stem (page 53)
isolated chain (page 63)
scalloping chain (page 64)
French knot (page 68)
lazy daisy (page 63)
fern (page 59)
cross (page 57)
threaded back stitch (page 54)
straight (no diagram—just single stitches)

COLORS USED:
All of them! For the fern stitches, the central vine was worked first in pale green and then the "leaves" were worked in bright green

Goofy Birds PILLOWCASE DRESS

I JUST COULDN'T RESIST whipping up some long-legged silly birds for your own little silly bird to wear. Pillowcase dresses have been a popular creation all by themselves for years, and are perfect for stitching. A quick look online will turn up numerous sources of patterns for making this dress, along with links offering pre-made versions.

STITCHES & SUPPLIES

TEXTILE:
See Resources (page 150) for pillowcase dresses.

PATTERN USED:
See transfer section for "Goofy Birds" template.

STITCHES USED:
back (page 54)
stem (page 53)
cross (page 57)
hidden (page 55)
French knot (page 68)
satin padded (page 61)
sheaf (page 70)
straight (no diagram-—just single stitches)

COLORS USED:
1010 medium yellow
1724 pale pink
2323 medium pink
2333 dark pink
3000 ivory
2615 violet

Robot Parts T-SHIRT

INSTEAD OF JUST PUTTING A ROBOT on the tykes' shirts (which they'd love) let's make *them* the robots! This is an easy transformation: just cover the front of a T-shirt with pattern of dials, switches, and important data. Beep boop beep!

STITCHES & SUPPLIES

TEXTILE:
Child's T-shirt

PATTERN USED:
See transfer section for "Robot Parts" template.

STITCHES USED:
back (page 54)

COLORS USED:
4636 bright green
1166 red
1010 medium yellow
1000 white
8705 dark gray
3822 bright blue

EXTRA SUPPLIES AND TOOLS:
You'll need to use a stabilizer for stitching on stretchy, knit fabric. See page 34 for information on stabilizers and see Resources (page 149) for suppliers.

Pocket Bluebird JEANS

WHY DO THE LEGS OF OUR JEANS get all the glory?
So often embroidery only appears down by the ankle or
on our derriere (both excellent places to put our stitches).
But your needlework will catch even more attention if you
embroider the front of your jeans, like I did: right where
your hands coolly rest in your pockets with some tattoo-
flash birdies.

   Stitching on denim can be a bear—see the techniques
for stitching on denim on page 31 for some helpful tips.

STITCHES & SUPPLIES

TEXTILE:
Your favorite jeans!

PATTERN USED:
See transfer section for
"Bluebird" template.

STITCHES USED:
split (page 52)
straight (no diagram-single
stitches used to outline
the beak)
hidden (page 55), on the
ribbon belt

COLORS USED:
3476 gray blue
3822 bright blue
1134 pale yellow
2323 medium pink
1000 white (on ribbon belt)

EXTRA SUPPLIES AND TOOLS:
I got some wide, pink ribbon
for a belt and edged it in a
hidden stitch.

Wild Western SHIRT

WESTERN WEAR AND WILD EMBROIDERY go together like needle and thread. The cut of Western shirts just seems to scream "Embroider me here! Embroider me there!" And c'mon, we all need at least one Western-cut shirt in our wardrobes. Don't deny your inner cowgirl. You can be subtle with your stitches, or go hog wild and hold nothing back. This is the time to break out the sequins and show off!

Western shirts are widely available new or as vintage wear and can be soft-spoken cottons or rope 'em–and– show 'em satins. Straight stitches are lined along the front yoke, imitating fringe (my favorite touch), while a pattern of pink leaves make a mosaic on the yoke and curling fern stitches entwine the collar. Cowboy poetry!

STITCHES & SUPPLIES

TEXTILE:
Western shirts abound at vintage clothing stores and re-sale shops. See Resources (page 150) for this custom-made Western shirt.

PATTERN USED:
See transfer section for "Leaf Shape" template.

STITCHES USED:
stem (page 53)
leaf (page 70)
fern (page 59)
back (page 54)
hidden (page 55)

COLORS USED:
3000 ivory
1724 pale pink
2323 medium pink
2333 dark pink
1010 medium yellow
4636 bright green

TECHNIQUES AND EXTRA EFFECTS:
Sequins (page 80)

Party Hostess APRON

SOMEONE AROUND HERE NEED A DRINK? The hostess herself just might. Let's be honest: we love the idea of vintage-style kitchen aprons more than we actually get to wear them. But there is another time when you can don a Donna Reed–style apron for fun: when you throw a party! Hostess aprons are meant to be silly, decorative, and thrown off once everyone's been served so you can pour yourself a drink and join the fun.

STITCHES & SUPPLIES

TEXTILE:
See Resources (page 150)
for aprons.

PATTERN USED:
See transfer section for
"Party Supplies" template.

STITCHES USED:
split (page 52)
stem (page 53)
back (page 54)
cross (page 57) (modified)
hidden (page 55)
straight (no diagram—
just single stitches)
traditional blanket (page 65)

COLORS USED:
1724 pale pink
2323 medium pink
4550 pale green
1134 pale yellow
8683 pale gray

**TECHNIQUES AND
EXTRA EFFECTS:**
Sequins (page 80)
metallic ribbon

Imitation Cameo BROOCH

WHAT BETTER USE OF THE SATIN STITCH than for a dark and lovely silhouette? This is a design you can stitch on the shoulder of a shirt for a trompe l'oeil cameo in embroidery. Charming!

If you look at the pattern for this project, you'll notice that I've divided this lovely lady into sections that will make your satin stitching simpler. It can be daunting to try and fill a large area effectively, and it helps to break it up into more manageable sections. And here's an idea for you: stitch each section in different directions for even greater textural effect. Everyone will admire your new heirloom!

STITCHES & SUPPLIES

TEXTILE:
Your own shirt

PATTERN USED:
See transfer section for "Silhouette" template.

STITCHES USED:
satin (page 61)
stem (page 53)
French knot (page 68)
straight (no diagram—just single stitches)

COLORS USED:
8705 dark gray
1724 pale pink
2606 pale violet

FINISHING TOUCHES

WANNA SHOW OFF?

◇◇◇◇◇◇◇◇◇◇◇◇◇◇◇◇◇◇◇◇◇◇◇◇

Framing · Cleaning

Show off your embroidery by

FINIS

HING
it right!

FRAMING

WANNA SHOW OFF? What to do if your embroidery project isn't conveniently located on some ready-to-wear textile? There are several ways you can display your embroidery. For who-knows-how-long, stitchers have used the hoop as the frame and hung it on the wall. They usually make use of an inexpensive wood hoop, gussied up with a lace edge added to the fabric peeking out from behind the hoop (the screw is usually visible too, or hidden with a pink bow). We've all seen one of these hanging somewhere, and it's synonymous with "Home Sweet Home" samplers. If hoop-as-frame is not really your favorite way to display embroidery on the wall, then here are some alternatives.

HOOP FRAMES:
These nifty hoops look more like picture frames than hoops, but they function as both. Offered in a range of sizes and shapes, you can paint and embellish them to match your project.

BANNERS:
I love banners, and they are my favorite way to display embroidery work. Readymade cotton banners are an option, or you can make your own. If you are cutting a piece of fabric to stitch on, leave excess at the bottom, sides, and top for hemming afterward—by hand or on a machine—with backing fabric. When finishing, I usually fold the top over and sew a sleeve for a hanging rod. Because your work isn't under glass you'll want to be picky about where you choose to display the banner, making sure it won't be exposed to any unwanted elements.

PROFESSIONAL FRAMING:
Be sure that whenever you opt to have your needlework professionally framed you seek out framers who are experienced with fabrics (look up quilting shops) and won't apply any solvents or adhesives, *of any kind*, to your work. That means no tape, spray adhesives, or sticky boards. Be aware that there is no such thing as "archival tape," even though it may be called that. If it sticks to your work, it's bad for your work. Needlework (as well as photos, prints, and other works of art that you care about) should be framed in such a way that your work can be removed from the frame without any damage to the piece. One way of doing this is by pinning the work to archival foamcore. The work will wrap around the square of foamcore (sized to the work and the frame), and stainless-steel pins are inserted into the edge of the foamcore, like furniture tacks, starting from the center out of each side. Then the excess fabric may be taped down on the back (if you don't care about what happens to the excess, that is). The older method of lacing your work across the back is no longer advisable as it's considered too stressful on the fabric. Another method is to suspend the work with thread passed once through the edge of the work, making an upward "V"

Embroidery Under Glass

WHENEVER YOUR WORK IS UNDER GLASS (or Plexiglas), it's very important that your work is spaced within the frame so the glass does not come into contact with the embroidery. Apart from keeping your stitches from being mashed down, this is to avoid any possible condensation forming inside the glass being wicked up by your work and becoming mildewy. Ew!

Location, Location, Location

A LOT OF OUR EMBROIDERY is a traveling display on our clothing, or found in our living rooms, bedrooms, and bathrooms. It's understood that these things will get used, handled, and lived with. And for the most part, our stitches can stand up to it. But if you've embroidered something that you care enough about to frame and display, you might care more about maintaining its condition. Kitchens and bathrooms are two of the worst places for displaying needlework because it will be exposed to extreme fluctuations in heat and humidity that cause fibers to expand and contract causing distortion, buckling, and distress to the fabric (not to mention the risk of water, oil, smoke, perfume, and various other things getting on them). These changes can take effect on your work immediately, not just over long periods of time. If you have just the perfect spot for your needlework in either of these rooms—which are favorites for displaying needlework—then I strongly advise keeping these works under glass. You'll be happy you did.

behind the edge of the window mat, where these threads are then taped down (and not the work—it's hanging by a thread, get it?). The method used will depend on the size and heft of the work, what's best for maintaining its condition, and your preferences.

DIY FRAMING:

Want to use a store-bought frame and just do it yourself? This is certainly an option, especially if you're not that protective of your work and just want to hang it on the wall already (or prop it up on a table among your family photos). Just be aware that most store-bought frames have a backing piece (the part you remove to put a picture in) made of acidic cardboard. It will be worth the extra few dollars to buy a piece of acid-free mat board to cut to size and layer between your work and the backing cardboard. Because a store-bought frame usually lacks the spacer that will keep your work from touching the glass, you might consider framing the piece with the glass removed.

LAUNDERING AND CARE

OVER THE YEARS, MANY PEOPLE HAVE ASKED me whether or not it's okay to toss that shirt they embroidered into the wash. Most of the time the answer is "yes." So long as you know that the floss is colorfast (won't bleed onto your shirt) and you take it easy with the dryer (which can make your work scrunch up), you should be fine. Your stitches should hold up and stay in place, unless they are extra long and loose. They won't come out in the wash, I promise.

IRONING VS. PRESSING:

Did you know there's a difference? Well, when it comes to really taking care of your textiles, there is. *Ironing* is when you "iron out" something, by simultaneously pressing and passing your iron over the fabric to smooth out wrinkles. When you do this, you're actually stretching out and distorting the weave and the fibers. That's not necessarily a bad thing, depending on what you're ironing. If your embroidery has gone a round in the dryer and scrunched up, you can dampen it and iron it again to regain its former shape, especially if the fabric is cotton, which is highly resilient. Iron the work on the backside, smoothing from the center out.

Pressing means that you press your iron and then lift it, replace it, and press. You don't smooth the iron across the surface when pressing. Again, if you can, press the backside to avoid any additional distortion of your stitches (or flattening of your French knots!).

HAND WASHING:
   If you're at all concerned about the sturdiness of your embroidered textile, do a hand-wash in a clean basin with lukewarm water and a fabric-friendly soap (see Resources, page 149). Skip the dryer this time, lay it flat, and press just before it's completely dry.

VACUUMING:
   Really? Yep! But hold up, don't lug your upright vacuum out of the closet for this job. Let's say you have an embroidered project with an inordinate amount of pet hair or dust accumulated on it. Sticky tape might pull precious fibers up and cause damage to the surface, so let's not go for that just yet. You can alleviate this unwanted layer without pulling and distorting your stitches in the process. Get a small amount of fiberglass mesh screen (more flexible than wire screen and available at most hardware stores) and lay it over the embroidery, holding it flat against its surface. Now, using a hand-held vacuum (the suction on an upright's extension is pretty intense, so opt for smaller vacs, like the one you use to clean your keyboard), vacuum over the screen mesh with the embroidery underneath. Dust comes up; your stitches don't.

Last but not least . . .

THE FINAL WORD

GET YOUR PROJECT STARTED!

◇◇◇◇◇◇◇◇◇◇◇◇◇◇◇◇◇◇◇◇◇◇◇◇◇◇◇◇◇◇◇◇◇◇

Transfer Patterns · Resources · Index

◇◇◇◇

Enough already, right? Okay, okay. Your transfer patterns are patiently awaiting your unbridled creativity. Remember that's what they're here for: *your* creativity. I hope the projects give you some ideas and inspiration instead of making you worry about perfectly reproducing them as they appear. And there are far more possibilities and ideas described than could ever be whipped up for projects in one book. I can't wait to see your own flights of stitching fancy take shape. After all, it's what you'll stitch on your own with these designs that will have the best effects! The embroidered possibilities are endless.

◇◇◇◇

TRANSFER PATTERNS

STEP 1: SET YOUR IRON TO ITS HOTTEST SETTING (or for Wool/Cotton). If your iron has a steam setting, make sure it is turned off. Steam, high humidity, and water will ruin the paper pattern and may blur the ink. You have been warned! While the iron is heating up, move on to the next step.

STEP 2: CAREFULLY TRIM AROUND THE PATTERN, making sure you leave some extra paper for your fingers or pins to anchor it down during ironing, to ensure that it won't shift. After you've cut out the pattern, play around with it to determine where you'd like to place it on your fabric. Even if it's just one single design, check it first. Imagine how it will look in that spot and if there's enough fabric in that area to go on your hoop, if you'll be using one. Done all that? Next step . . .

STEP 3: PREHEAT YOUR FABRIC by ironing it before you place the pattern on the fabric. By preheating the fabric, you ensure that the dye from the transfer will take more easily, and you'll smooth out any wrinkles. Cool fabric may not take the transfer ink very easily, no matter how hot your iron is. Many people skip this step—don't be one of them! Keep your fabric warm while imprinting.

STEP 4: PLACE A PIECE OF SCRAP CLOTH UNDER THE FABRIC you're imprinting so that the pattern doesn't pass through the weave and imprint on what's underneath it—like the cover on your ironing board. Maybe you don't care, but I would. And don't say I didn't warn you! Position the pattern, ink-side down, where you want it to appear on the fabric.

STEP 5: IRON THE PATTERN, holding it in place on the fabric and trying to cover the entire pattern with the iron at once to distribute the ink evenly. Make sure the pattern doesn't shift when the iron moves! The harder you press and the more you iron, the darker the design will appear (and the more ink you'll use, resulting in fewer re-applications of the transfers). Gotta peek? Be sure to do so by turning back the pattern edge without shifting the pattern. If the lines are too faint for you to follow, just keep on ironing. It shouldn't take more than ten firm passes of the iron to get a decent imprint. If the pattern still appears too faint, make sure the iron is sufficiently hot and that your fabric is still warm.

Remember, you can use the pattern more than once. Place the design again on your fabric in a new location, or just set it aside and save it for another project.

RESOURCES

I'VE TRIED TO COMPILE as many helpful resources mentioned in the text as possible to lead you to more designs, stitch diagrams, and sources for tools, textiles, and threads used in the projects.

SOURCES FOR SUPPLIES

Iron-on transfers, carbon paper, stabilizer, textiles, hoops (and hoop frames), scissors, glow-in-the-dark threads, metallic threads, and more are available from the author's company, Sublime Stitching: *www.SublimeStitching.com*

Please take time to discover your local, independently owned needlework shop! These specialty boutiques may stock many of the supplies listed here (and they can show you in person how to work a stitch that has you stumped).

MISCELLANEOUS

Needle In A Haystack (platinum needles and more): *www.needlestack.com*

Q-Snap Frames (PVC square frames): *www.qsnap.com*

Quilters Warehouse (needle grabbers): *www.quilterswarehouse.com*

STABILIZERS AND TRANSFER PENS

www.sulky.com

STENCILS

www.quiltingstencils.com

SILICONE THREAD CONDITIONER

Thread Heaven (available from numerous online sources)

TEXTILE WASH

Soak: *www.soakwash.com*

MORE PATTERNS, INSTRUCTIONS, AND SOURCES

AMH Design: *www.amhdesignonline.com*

Aunt Martha's Colonial Patterns: *www.colonialpatterns.com*

Feeling Stitchy: *www.feelingstitchy.com*

Jenny Henry Needlepoint: *www.jennyhenrydesigns.com*

Needlecrafter: *www.needlecrafter.com*

Needle 'n Thread: *www.needlenthread.com*

Pattern Bee: *www.patternbee.com*

Primrose Design: *www.primrosedesign.com*

Wee Wonderfuls: *www.weewonderfuls.typepad.com*

THREADS:

Crescent Colours (silks and overdyed threads): *www.crescentcolours.com*

Kreinik (metallics and iron-on threads): *www.kreinik.com*

Presencia (stranded floss): *www.presenciausa.com*

Rainbow Gallery (metallic ribbon): *www.rainbowgallery.com*

TEXTILES USED IN PROJECTS:

Cotton shower curtain on page 95: *www.antiquehardware.com*

Kimono on page 119: *www.personalizationmall.com*

Laptop case pattern and fabric on page 107 by Amy Butler: *www.amybutlerdesign.com*

Party Hostess Apron on page 135: *www.sublimestitching.com*

Pillowcase dress on page 127 by Babies Momma Shop: *www.etsy.com*

Tablecloth on page 93, and wrap skirt on page 125: *www.dharmatrading.com*

Western Shirt on page 133 by Kathie Sever: *www.ramonsterwear.com*

Work shirt on page 121: *www.dickies.com*

Zippered pillowcase on page 97: *www.sublimestitching.com*

FAVORITE BOOKS ON EMBROIDERY *(Many of these are out of print, but can still be found used online.)*

Day, Lewis F., *Art In Needlework*. New York: Charles Scribner's Sons, 1901.

Howard, Constance, *The Constance Howard Book of Stitches*. London: Batsford, 1979.

Mackenzie, Althea, *Embroideries*. London: The National Trust, 2004.

McMorris, Penny, *Crazy Quilts*. New York: E.P. Dutton, Inc., 1984.

Norden, Mary, *Decorative Embroidery*. Pleasantville, New York: Reader's Digest, 1997.

Wilson, Erica, *Erica Wilson's Embroidery Book*. New York: Charles Scribner's Sons, 1973.

BOOKS WITH DIAGRAMS FOR LEFTIES

Montano, Judith Baker, *Elegant Stitches: An Illustrated Stitch Guide and Source Book of Inspiration*. Lafayette, California: C&T Publishing, 1995.

Svennas, Elsie and Petersen, Grete, *Handbook of Stitches*. New York: Van Nostrand Reinhold Company, 1970.

THE AUTHOR WOULD LIKE TO GRATEFULLY ACKNOWLEDGE those sources of higher authority she consulted during her research in writing this book:

Bond, Dorothy, *Crazy Quilt Stitches*. Cotton Grove, Oregon: Dorothy Bond, 1981.

Brown, Pauline. *The Encyclopedia of Embroidery Techniques*. New York: Viking Studio, 1994.

Dunnewold, Jane. *Complex Cloth: A Comprehensive Guide to Surface Design*. Bothell, Washington: That Patchwork Place, Inc., 1996.

Montano, Judith. *The Crazy Quilt Handbook*. Lafayette, California: C&T Publishing, 2001.

Riley, Lesley. *Quilted Memories: Journaling, Scrapbooking & Creating Keepsakes with Fabric*. New York: Sterling/Chapelle, 2005.

Thomas, Mary. *Mary Thomas's Dictionary of Embroidery Stitches*. New York: Crescent Books, 1989.

The embroidered screen door project the author refers to on page 32 can be found in *Craftivity*, by Tsia Carson, available from HarperCollins.

The image used on the señorita card on page 109 is called "Istmeña" (artist unknown) as it appears in *Mexican Calendar Girls*, available from Chronicle Books.

ACKNOWLEDGMENTS

THANKS AND HEARTFELT APPRECIATION are owed to countless people who have supported Sublime Stitching over the years, especially:

My mom, always.

Mary McIlravy, Jessica Olsen, Jordan Lee, and Krystal Wyatt-Baxter, who make every day at Sublime Stitching a joy and a dream realized.

Andrea Jenkinson and Scott Cronk, for their continued, invaluable guidance and illuminating advice.

Ginger Edwards and Liz Napier, for their kind mentorship as needleworkers and generous sharing of information.

"My Gal" Alicia Traveria, for her flawless abilities with graphics production.

My agent, Stacey Glick, for her dedicated hard work, incredible patience, and unwavering good humor.

My editor, Kate Woodrow, and designer, Aya Akazawa, for their creative contributions, hard work, and kind attention to my numerous concerns. Thanks also to Ann Spradlin, Doug Ogan, Yolanda Accinelli, Nancy Deane, and the other wonderful people at Chronicle Books for making such considerable efforts on my behalf in supporting my vision and voice.

Jessica Vitkus, for letting me know she's there when I need her.

Teresa Errington, for generously advising me on framing techniques.

Also to David Zellner, Faythe Levine, Doug Kreinik, Jeane Hutchins, Christy Petterson, Debbie Stoller, Natalie Zee Drieu, Dale Dougherty, Sherry Huss, Jenny Ryan, Leah Kramer, Jen Hazen, William Haugh, Yvonne and Josh Lambert, Aide Uzgiris, Mindy and Marin Briggs, Kenny Gall, Mr. Jalopy, Mark Frauenfelder, Mitch O'Connell, Julie Hoelscher, Domy Books, Chad Herring, Aubrey Edwards, Divya Srinivasan, Okay Mountain, Yard Dog Folk Art, Amy Schroeder, Shannon Okey, the Austin Craft Mafia, and, of course, the Glitterati.

Special thanks go to the following women who generously lent their time and skills helping stitch projects for this book. Without their contributions, this book would not have been possible. I am also indebted to each of them for their incredibly kind and sustaining support of Sublime Stitching:

Amy Bindel (projects on pages: 95, Fan Dancer Shower Curtain; 121, Tattoo Heart on Your Sleeve; 131, Pocket Bluebird Jeans)

Ginger Edwards (projects on pages: 119, Funky Sashiko Kimono; 123, Peacock Bomber Jacket; 135, Party Hostess Apron; 137, Imitation Cameo Brooch)

Flor Hernandez (projects on pages: 103, Chandelier Magnets; 125, Mexican Sugar Skulls Wrap Skirt; 127, Goofy Birds Pillowcase Dress)

Rachel Hobson (projects on pages: 93, Mahjong table cloth; 107, Amy Butler Laptop Case; 113, Felt Flower Bouquet; 129, Robot Parts T-Shirt)

All other projects were stitched by the author, including, in part, those on page 113 (Felt Flower Bouquet) and page 135 (Party Apron).

Thanks also to Leslie Bonnell for her sewing skills on the hostess apron and laptop case, Kathie Sever for providing one of her wonderful custom-made Western shirts, and Chrissy Paszalek for being a last-minute seamstress extraordinaire.

STITCH SAMPLER MAP

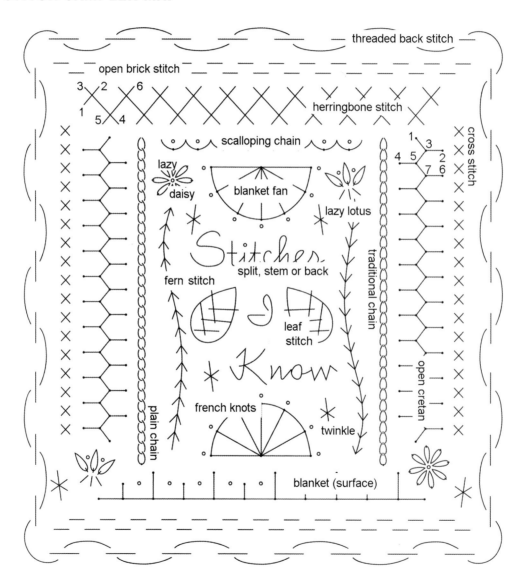

INDEX

LEAF TEMPLATE
(do not iron these words)

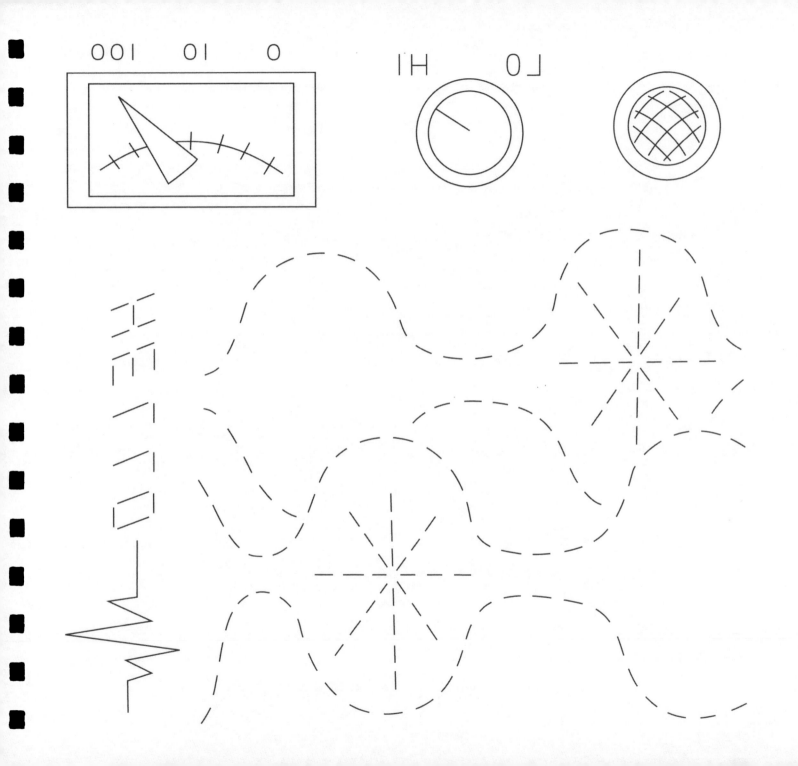